# Racial Realism and the History of Black People in America

# Racial Realism and the History of Black People in America

Lori Latrice Martin

LEXINGTON BOOKS
*Lanham • Boulder • New York • London*

Published by Lexington Books
An imprint of The Rowman & Littlefield Publishing Group, Inc.
4501 Forbes Boulevard, Suite 200, Lanham, Maryland 20706
www.rowman.com
6 Tinworth Street, London SE11 5AL, United Kingdom

Copyright © 2022 The Rowman & Littlefield Publishing Group, Inc.

Chapter 4: parts of this chapter were previously publish in *American in Denial* (2021), Albany, NY: SUNY Press and are used with permission.
Conclusion: parts of this chapter were previously published in *America in Denial* (2021), Albany, NY: SUNY Press and are used with permission.

*All rights reserved.* No part of this book may be reproduced in any form or by any electronic or mechanical means, including information storage and retrieval systems, without written permission from the publisher, except by a reviewer who may quote passages in a review.

**British Library Cataloguing in Publication Information Available**

**Library of Congress Cataloging-in-Publication Data Available**

ISBN 978-1-7936-4816-7 (cloth)
ISBN 978-1-7936-4817-4 (electronic)

# Contents

| | |
|---|---|
| Acknowledgments | vii |
| Introduction | 1 |
| Chapter One: The Genius of Derrick Bell: Racial Realism | 21 |
| Chapter Two: Forty Acres and a Mule and Other Missed Opportunities | 45 |
| Chapter Three: The Myth of the Greatest Generation | 67 |
| Chapter Four: (Un)Civil Rights and Black Power | 83 |
| Chapter Five: Promises Unfulfilled: Black Lives Matter Chatter | 103 |
| Conclusion: Racism, COVID-19, and Election 2020 | 117 |
| References | 125 |
| Index | 139 |
| About the Author | 147 |

# Acknowledgments

I wish to acknowledge all the love and support that I received from my mother, Edith Jean Burns, over the course of my life. She was my superpower. I will forever miss her presence. I also wish to acknowledge the love and support from my father, Lee Edward Burns, Sr., that is the wind beneath my wings. I am forever grateful for my sons, Emir Sykes, and Derrick Martin, Jr. I would also like to express my appreciation for the individuals and organizations that have sown into my life and to those who assisted me in getting through this book project during a particularly difficulty time. Thank you: Lee Burns, Jr., Constance Slaughter Harvey, Constance Harvey, Burwell and Family, Stephen C. Finley, Clovier Torry, Lois Edmonds, LSU Athletics, ABIS, Dorothea Swann, Emily Thornton, John Thornton, Rachel Nichols, Brent Chambliss, Shanille Thomas, Mary Hilliard, Nyack Library, Frances Pratt, Chandra Joseph, Landon Douglass, Tat Yau, J'Ara Anthony Righteous Rogers, Lynette Cotto, Derrick Lathan, Hayward Derrick Horton, Mark Naison, Henry Louis Taylor, John Sibley Butler, Maretta McDonald, Dominque Dillard, Mahalia Howard, Derrick Lathan, LSU Department of African and African American Studies, LSU College of Humanities and Social Sciences, Andre Sigmone, Eugene Jones, Sr., Rockland County Ministers Alliance, Baptists Ministers Evening Conference of New York City and Greater Vicinity, Greater St. Johns COGIC, Raymond Jetson, Eldon Birthwright, Tony Brown, Wil Glover, Chris and Sonya Williams, Dione Footman, Derrick Martin, Doris Spencer, David and Shannon Rudder, Jeffrey Murphy, Timothy Roscoe, Patrick Thomas, Parco Cosey, Michael Jenkins, Courtney Morales, Shelby Russell, and the editorial staff at Lexington Books.

# Introduction

Race remains one of the most significant determinants of black people in America. Race determines one's life chances and opportunities. For black people that has meant fewer life chances and opportunities. Black people have tried to combat the antiblackness that has characterized their existence in America since the first group of kidnapped Africans were brought to Jamestown, Virginia, in 1619. At various times in American history, black people felt a sense of hopefulness and optimism that America would finally extend treasured American values to them. History shows that black people have had their expectations raised so many times only to find themselves deeply disappointed. Dr. Eddie Glaude, Professor of African American Studies at Princeton University, provides the best explanation for understanding the experience of black people in America in his defense of Dr. Cornel West, Professor of the Practice of Public Philosophy at Harvard University and Professor Emeritus at Princeton University, and West's criticisms of former President Barack Obama. Like West, black people in America have been duped, explained Glaude (2016) in his book *Democracy in Black*. They have been assured of inclusion and assimilation into mainstream society only to find themselves marginalized time and time again. In addition to Glaude's insights, Derrick Bell's, a Professor of Law at Harvard University and one of the founders of critical race theory, work on racial realism is very important. Bell (1992) makes the argument that black people should not seek redress from the American court system or from other American social institutions because the legal system and other American social institutions are structured in such a way to reinforce the permanent subordination of black people in America. Bell's (1992) views might seem unpopular and pessimistic to some people, but his perspective is both historically accurate and realistic.

One need only look at America's past and the ongoing racial disparities between black and white people in America for evidence to support Bell's (1992) contention that black people are perpetually living at the bottom of the well.

The evidence that black people have been and remain at the bottom of racialized American social structure may be found in many places. Cohen et al. (2006) conducted research on the racial achievement gap. The scholars explored how a social-psychological intervention might reaffirm a sense of personal adequacy for black students. Specifically, Cohen et al. (2006) used a class-based writing assignment aimed at allowing black students to see themselves as good, virtuous, and efficacious, and the result was improved grades. The emphasis on self-integrity for black students was effective in combating the negative stereotype threats to black students in school settings.

Pedro Noguera (2008) also studied racial achievement gaps, which are often measured as disparities in test scores and academic outcomes. Noguera (2008) showed how historically, intelligence was regarded as an innate property. It was one of many genetic endowments and members of the dominant racial group in America did not believe that black people were very intelligent. Consequently, there was a widely held belief that black children were not as intelligent or as capable as white children. This way of thinking is still with us, argued Noguera (2008), and is especially visible in discussions about the racial achievement gap. What has happened today more recently was that biological arguments about the inferiority of black intelligence were replaced by cultural arguments. Black children did not perform as well as white children because they embraced an opposition culture or that they saw education as a form of forced assimilation. Noguera (2008), cited other claims that black children embraced a culture of anti-intellectualism or a victimology where white people were the source of their problems. Still others, Noguera (2008) said, pointed to a broader culture of poverty that hindered the academic success of black children when compared with white children. Noguera (2008) conducted a case study of two school districts and was able to identify a number of factors that contribute to the ongoing racial achievement gap. Black children often have less access to rigorous courses, mentoring, and counseling. They often have limited access to educational leaders that are transformational and committed to addressing the needs of black students. Noguera (2008) also found that the failure to link the racial academic gap with broader social issues such as racial disparities income, wealth, parent education, access to health care, good paying jobs, and vital social services contribute to the enduring racial achievement gap.

Pritchard and Wiatrowsi (2008) provide further evidence of the disadvantages that black people have faced historically and continue to face in more recent time. The scholars focused on race and capital punishment at the state level. They found that states with higher concentrations of black citizens and conservative populations and political elites, primarily in the South, were more likely to have a higher number of prisoners on death row and were more likely to execute a higher number of those prisoners. For example, states with the highest executions between 1977 and 1996, were Texas with 107, Florida with 38, and Virginia with 37. The states with the highest under sentence were

California (454), Texas (438), and Florida (373). Pritchard and Wiatrowski (2008) were able to show that race and ideology at the state level was influential at each stage of the death penalty process.

Thomas Shapiro is well-known for his work on racial wealth inequality. He published a study with several of his colleagues examining racial wealth inequality over time. Shapiro et al. (2013) found that over a twenty-five-year period that the white-black wealth gap nearly tripled. It was $85,000 in 1984 and more than $236,000 by 2009. The researchers found that the driving forces behind the racial wealth gap were years of homeownership, household income, unemployment, college education, and inheritance. Shapiro and his co-authors found unequal wealth rewards for white and black people.

Collins et al. (2019) work on the racial wealth gap further highlighted the permanent subordination of black people in America. Wealth, like few other measures, captures the cumulative and intergenerational effects of historic and contemporary racial inequities. Collins and colleagues found that between 1983 and 2016, for example, that the median black family wealth dropped by half compared to a 33 percent increase for white families. Black families were twenty times more likely to have zero or negative wealth (37 percent) than they were to have $1 million or more in assets (1.9 percent). White families were equally likely to have zero or negative wealth as they were to be a millionaire (15 percent/15 percent). The authors concluded that changing individual behavior was not the answer to closing the racial wealth gap. Among their race-specific solutions, the authors called for a congressional committee on reparations and improved collection of data on race and wealth.

Many other scholars have studied persistent racial wealth inequalities and the lasting effects on generations of black people. Semega et al. (2020) found that the median income for non-Hispanic white households was about $76,000 compared to about $45,440 for black households. Between 1967 and 2019, Semega's et al. (2020) research showed that black households had the lowest real median income in each year. Their work also showed that the poverty rate for white households was 7.3 compared to nearly nineteen for black households.

Compton and his colleagues researched racial and ethnic health disparities, especially as they related to COVID-19. Their research also supported claims of the subordination of black people. Compton et al. (2020) studied the social determinants of racial disparities in health with an emphasis on neighborhoods and the physical environment. They examined housing, transportation, crowding, and lack of access to quality health care. They also considered occupation and job conduction, income and wealth, and education. Compton et al. (2020) found that black people were overrepresented in essential work settings and that they have lower incomes, lower wealth levels, and more debt than white people. Lower literacy and more barriers to higher education also made black people more vulnerable COVID-19 than other groups. Black people, according to Compton et al. (2020), had higher rates of COVID-19 infection, hospitalization, and death.

Zelner et al. (2020) also examined the relationship between race and COVID-19. Specifically, the scholars estimated COVID-19 incidence and mortality by race and ethnicity. They found that black people experienced the most confirmed and probable COVID-19 cases and died disproportionately. Variation in household, community, and workplace exposure were among the determining factors not case-fatality rates.

Alkon et al. (2020) joined other scholars in conducting research that examined potential links between race and COVID-19. The researchers explored diet-related health conditions and where they placed some people, namely black people for whom food justice is an issue, at greater risk than other racial and ethnic groups. Alkon et al. (2020) did find that race mattered and cautioned against efforts to conceptualize the challenge as the consequence of individual choice as was often the case in popular culture and nutrition science. Instead, Alkon et al. (2020), like other food justice researchers, understand that racialized structural issues affect food consumption.

Lieberman-Cribbin et al. (2020) studied racial disparities in COVID-19 testing and positivity in New York City. The researchers found that the number of total tests significantly increased with the increasing proportion of white residents. They also found that the ratio of positive tests significantly decreased with the increasing proportion of white residents in the zip code. Lieberman-Cribbin et al. (2020) concluded that testing in New York City was not proportional to need and this may be the case in other areas.

Additional research has been conducted that focused on racial health disparities and the terrible outcomes for black people in America when compared with other groups, especially when compared with individuals with membership in the dominant racial group. Fong et al. (2020) studied race, birth weight, and neighborhood polarization in Massachusetts. The researchers analyzed data from 2001 through 2013 and found health disparities by race. Likewise, Goldberg et al. (2020) looked at the role of race in understanding health care and mental health outcomes. The authors of the study focused on military service. They found that among civilians, racial minorities had a longer time to PTSD and depression treatment initiation. They also found no difference among veterans, PTSD and depression with respect to treatment initiation but shorter time to treatment initiation for black veterans for alcohol-use disorder treatment. Goldberg et al. (2020) observed greater barriers to treatment initiation for black people in the study was due to economic injustices and disparities in access to health care. Access to the

Veterans Health Administration and Tricare addressed some of the observed racial disparities present in the civilian population.

Sakhuja et al. (2021) examined racial disparities in colorectal cancer screening with and without cardiovascular disease. They looked at data in 15 states from 2012 to 2016. The researchers showed that whites and Hispanics with a history of heart disease were more likely to undergo colorectal cancer screening than black respondents. Sakhuja et al. (2021) called for improved screening for black people to narrow the racial gap.

The disadvantages that black people experience in health when compared with white people were evidence across the life course. Taylor et al. (2020) used cumulative inequality theory to examine racial disparities in impairment as individuals approached death. The theory holds "that social systems produce inequality in multiple domains that begin early in life, such as racial minority status and other early life markers of disadvantage such as poverty, to produce differential exposure as individuals age" (Taylor et al. 2020, 1293). They analyzed data from North Carolina. The study findings revealed significant black-white disparities among older adults as they approach death and that the differences were not fully mediated by socioeconomic state. Black people were even disadvantaged on the lesser known issue of energy poverty. Wang et al. (2021) examined data from 1990, 1997, 2005, and 2015, and found that black people were more vulnerable than other groups.

Although some people mistakenly see sports purely as a source of entertainment, sports also provide some of the best evidence of the persistent low status of black people in America. This is especially true when one looks at various aspects related to the black college athlete experience, especially the experiences of black men in and around the high-revenue generating teams. Harper (2016) published a study about the relative disadvantages that black people experienced in college sports over the past few years. Harper (2016) found that while black men accounted for 2.5 of all undergraduates at NCAA Division 1 institutions, they accounted for over 56 percent of the football players and almost 61 percent of the basketball players. In the Power 5 conferences, only about 16 percent of all head coaches were black men. All of the Athletic Directors were white, at the time of Harper's study. Harper (2016) also compared the graduate rates of black men athletes in NCAA Division 1 College sports and found the low rates at Kansas State (26 percent), Michigan State (33 percent), Oklahoma State (33 percent), University of Mississippi (33 percent), University of Iowa (34 percent), and University of California-Berkeley (34 percent). Harper (2016) highlighted further just how overrepresented black men athletes were at some NCAA Division 1 schools. In the Southeastern Conference (SEC), for example, the difference between the percentages of black men among all undergraduates and the percentages of black men in Men's Basketball and Football were in many cases over 70 percent. For example, black men accounted for 3.2 percent of all undergraduate students, nearly 78 percent of players on the teams identified previous with a difference of about 74.7 percent. The difference between black men as a percentage of all undergrads and the percentage of black men on Men's Basketball and Football teams was 72.2 percent for Mississippi State, 71.5 percent for University of Mississippi, 70.7 percent for Texas A&M, and 66.5 percent for the University of Alabama.

Additionally, Harper's (2016) research revealed lower graduate rates for black men athletes when compared to all athletes expect in a few cases. The graduate rate at the University of Florida was 43 percent for black men athletes and 86 percent for all students. At the University of Mississippi, the graduate rate for black men athletes was 33 percent compared to 60 percent for all students. At the University of Georgia, the graduate rate for black men athletes was a little over 50 percent and 84 percent for all students. Harper (2016) cited a lack of transparency as an ongoing issue and called for money from championships to support programming. Harper (2016) also called for targeted advising and for setting racial equality goals where the hiring of black coaches was concerned. Moreover, Harper (2016) called upon the media to change the single-narratives and one-sided portrayals of black college athletes so that black families would have an easier time helping their children understand that most grassroots and college athletes go pro in something other than sports.

Cunningham (2021) took a deeper dive into the connection between race and sports as it related to coaching. To place the issue of racism and coaching in a broader context, Cunningham (2021) observed that only fifteen African Americans have ever served as CEOs in the entire history of the Fortune 500. He also noted that in the NCAA Women's Basketball, racial minorities were nearly four times more likely to be players than they were to serve as a head coach. Cunningham (2021) cited discrimination in coaching and administration. Cunningham (2021) contended that the explanations are multilevel. Institutional racism, stakeholder concerns, bias in decision-making, organization, culture and practices were among the identified causes for the relative marginalization of black people as coaches in college sports.

Dixon (2020) conducted research on the history of education in Mississippi to shed light on current racial disparities in the state and beyond. Dixon (2020) outlined how so-called freedom of choice plans served as stall tactics to prevent Mississippi and other states from integrating schools as called for by the U.S. Supreme Court and lower courts. Dixon (2020) observed that "just as quickly as schools desegregated in Mississippi, schools were resegregating" (3), and this was happening in other states, especially across the South. Dixon (2020) called for vouchers for early education for black children as a remedy. Dixon (2020) also recommended additional funding for schools with high black student enrollments and free tuition through the bachelor's degree and no standardized test requirements.

Kang (2021) showed how racial disparities in education persist even beyond the pursuit of undergraduate degree through earned doctorates. Nearly 5,500 black people earned doctorates in 2019 out of the total number of doctorate recipients which was just over 55,700. Black people who earned doctorates were also more likely to earn them in non-science and engineering fields like psychology and other social sciences.

Since the May 25, 2020, killing of George Floyd, many college athletes have used their platform to draw attention to racial inequities, especially police involved shootings. Headley and Wright (2020) focused on racial disparities in the use of force and arrests. Using data from New Orleans collected between 2016 and 2019, the pair found that black officers were less likely to use higher levels of force on black civilians than white officers but both black and white officers were less likely to arrest white civilians in use of force encounters. The unequal treatment black people receive in these types of engagement with law enforcement are also evidence of the historic and contemporary subordinate status of black people. "Scholars conclude that police brutality against people of color is one of the most significant unfulfilled goals of the civil rights movement" (Wright 2020, 1).

Mentch (2020) also studied race and fatal police shootings using data from January 2015 through July 2016 from five national databases, including from the Census, FBI, and Department of Justice. Mentch (2020) investigated racial distributions of shootings. Mentch (2020) found that "not only is the proportion of Black victims 'significantly' different from local racial demographics, but that the total number of Black police shooting victims is more than nineteen standard deviations larger than expected" (16).

While the architects of America's most important documents never intended to include black people, many black people, nonetheless, believed that they should. Evidence of the belief that black people treasured the ideals of democracy, fairness, justice, and equality for all can be found in black people's participation in every significant war. Black people fought alongside the very people who were oppressing them during the American Revolution. Indeed, patriots, as white people were called who fought for their independence from Great Britain, likened their exploitation and unequal treatment to the treatment of enslaved people in America. Not wanting to have their images and destinies controlled by a foreign empire, patriots fought for their freedom at the same time they held an entire group of people in physical bondage. Despite the hypocrisy, black people fought for the cause of liberty only to find that they remained largely in bondage and would remain so for nearly a hundred more years.

Black people were also on the front lines of the American Civil War. While white people, especially in the South, fought to maintain the system of slavery in America, black people joined the Union Army for their own liberation and for that of the divided nation. The eventual end to the Civil War held out a great deal of promise that the nation was entering a new area. Reconstruction brought with it many promises that unfortunately were unfulfilled and elude the grasp of the vast majority of black people today.

Among the many American men and women fighting during the World Wars of the twentieth century were black soldiers. They fought against racism and fascism abroad and at home. They fought to secure rights and freedoms that they could not enjoy in the country they and their ancestors helped build. Nevertheless, black people, through their service in the armed forces, consistently showed a strong belief in the promise that America would one day include them as part of the nation's vision. Despite their valiant service, some black people were more hailed for their service by foreign countries than by their own.

The unequal treatment that black people received compared to white people in America was of course not relegated to their military service but extended to all areas of American life. Black people were limited in their abilities to learn to read and write for a time in American history. Doing so could be punishable by a fine or even incarceration. Once educational opportunities were opened to black people they were by and large underfunded both in terms of the amount of money spent per pupil and in the wages for black teachers.

While black people longed to own land and were promised greater access to land and other forms of ownership after legally no longer being considered assets themselves, many public policies and private practices were put in place to make sure that the dreams of ownership would not become a reality for the majority of black people. After the Civil War, black people were not allowed forty acres or the use of old government mules. Many black people were caught up in a discriminatory system of sharecropping that kept them and their offspring forever indebted to the landowner. Still other black people found themselves the victims of Draconian rules that lead to incarceration and provided the labor for a profitable convict leasing scheme. White owned companies and/or white lead Sheriff's Departments and the communities they served would benefit monetarily by using the labor of incarcerated individuals who were serving time for any number of criminalized behaviors, including but not limited to vagrancy.

Black people were also kept out of one of the greatest periods of wealth accumulation in America. The first half of the twentieth century saw average white Americans own homes for the first time in the country's history. Prior to the 1930s, private homeownership was out of the reach of most Americans. Only the truly rich could afford a home. In order to own a home before the

1940s, it was required that the buyer pay at least half of the price of the home. Additionally, the buyer would have a relatively short time to pay off the remaining balance. With the establishment of the Home Owner's Loan Corporation and the Federal Housing Administration homeownership became more accessible to the average American—the average white American. The federal agencies would underwrite loans so that buyers could put down very little as a down payment on a home and have as many as thirty years to pay off the balance. This period resulted in one of the largest mass accumulations of wealth in America, again, for white America because black people were not granted the same access to homeownership as white people. Through the practices of the federal government, financial institutions, and private citizens, black people were left out and left behind. Black people had hoped that they too could leave behind crowded urban areas for life in the newly formed suburbs only to find that the suburbs were off limits to them.

It is almost unimaginable for some today, but black people also experienced the disappointment of not being able to enjoy some of the very activities that white people enjoyed like swimming in public pools or sitting anywhere on a public bus. The City of Baton Rouge in Louisiana is a good example of this history. For a time in the first few decades of the 1900s, city pools were off limits to black people in Baton Rouge even though their tax dollars funded them. Some white people did not want black people swimming in the pool with them for fear that their diseased bodies might contaminate the water and thus sicken healthy white bodies or that the color line would become blurred and black and white people might consider miscegenation no longer taboo. After a summer of sweltering heat that led to the drowning of more than one black child seeking relief from the heat in a watering hole he happened along, black residents met to discuss their next moves. Some black residents wanted to force the integration of the pool. Other black residents did not think integrating the pool would be successful and called for the creation of a pool and park of their own. Black residents of Baton Rouge did the latter. They pooled their resources and built their own swimming pool and park, naming it after a local man, Brooks Park.

By the early 1950s, black people in Baton Rouge, like black people in other cities and towns, found themselves riding in the backs of buses. In many of these cities, black people made up the majority of the ridership. They paid the same fare as white riders but were forced to sit in the back away from the driver, who was almost always white and male, and the white passengers. This was the case even when there were no white riders on the bus. Growing tired of seeing half empty buses with mostly black men, women, and children sitting and standing in the back, the black community in Baton Rouge met and was able to get the City Council to agree to an ordinance, Ordinance 222, which would permit seating on a first come, first serve basis. Unfortunately, the white men bus drivers refused to enforce the ordinance and with the backing of a statewide official the ordinance was declared in violation of segregation laws. Black people in Baton Rouge refused to ride the buses after the State supported the white men bus drivers and their threatened strike. The black people of Baton Rouge developed a car rider sharing system. The system included several stops strategically located in the city where black people could get rides to work and other places they needed to go and not have to rely on public transportation.

For about a week, the Baton Rouge Bus Boycott continued. It ended with a compromise that resulted in the front seats reserved for white riders and the back seat reserved for black riders and the seats in the middle were for available to riders on a first come, first serve basis. The car share was one of the most important aspects of the boycott. It is therefore not surprising that it was one of the things that the architects of the Montgomery Bus Boycott adopted in their protests that lasted more than a year and began in 1955. Despite the sacrifices of the black people of Baton Rouge and later the black people of Montgomery, Alabama, black people would continue to have to fight to be treated as human beings with all of the rights and benefits associated with citizenship in America. Any hope that black people had that this would happen after direct actions at public pools and on public transportation were short-lived.

Scholars, including Aldon Morris, have written about the civil rights movement. While the civil rights movement that is associated with Dr. Martin Luther King, Jr., was part of a longer struggle for basic human and civil rights, it could be argued that it started in the 1950s with the *Brown v. Board of Education* ruling, or the killing of fourteen-year old Emmet Till, or the Montgomery Bus Boycott. The precise origins notwithstanding, the civil rights movement was hailed then and is still cheered now by some for several important legislative victories. The passage of the Civil Rights Act of 1964, the Voting Rights Act of 1965, and the Fair Housing Act of 1968, were viewed as key pieces of legislation that would finally do for black people what the Reconstruction period that followed the Civil War did not and could not do. These three pieces of legislation were supposed to finally provide black people with access to public accommodations, voting, and housing. While celebrated as a sort of Second Reconstruction, the new laws did little to improve the quality of life for the majority of black people. Indeed, the civil rights movement has been critiqued by many scholars and others by focusing too much on the goodness of the legal system and issues that disproportionately benefited middle-class black people, and not enough on the plight of more economically disadvantaged black people. The leaps and bounds of black progress many anticipated did not manifest and black people as a group were again left feeling duped.

If there were any questions about where black people stood after the 1960s, they were answered with the backlash that resulted and was made plain in efforts to reverse affirmative actions to address racial inequities in America. *Bakke v. University of California Board of Regents* (1978) was just one example. Antiblack sentiments were increasingly clocked in color-blind rhetoric. There were calls to end programs where race was considered for the purpose of addressing past wrongs enacted by members of the dominant racial group in America against nonwhite groups and women, including black people. In the *Bakke* case, admissions standards were on trial as was America's commitment to creating a more equitable and a more just society where race was concerned. The majority of America, the majority of white America, made it clear that they did not support efforts to right America's wrongs and also did not want to be held responsible for the sins of their mothers and fathers. This unwillingness to reckon with race had many consequences. It left black people again feeling that they had misplaced their hope in the ethical and moral character of the majority of Americans. The lack of commitment to address the effects of the legacy of race and racism on black people in more contemporary times made it easier to blame black people for their own circumstances and to continue to see black people as a whole as lacking humanity.

The inability to see that black lives did matter, and that black people were deserving of the same rights and privileges of white people in America made it increasingly possible to dehumanize and criminalize blackness and black people. Among the consequences were wars on poverty and drugs that led to the mass incarceration of mostly black men. Black men increasingly became the fuel for a profitable prison industrial complex that made once struggling rural white communities suddenly economically viable. Black people were duped into thinking that the nation was concerned about their overrepresentation among the poor and the threats that an influx of illegal substances was having on their community only to learn that they were considered members of the undeserving poor. They were blamed for their relatively low socioeconomic status. It was a culture of poverty not a system of oppression that left many black people living in poverty. This culture of poverty also contributed to a breakdown in social norms, some criminologist argued, which led to high incarceration not the increased surveillance of predominately black communities.

For the next few decades black people would have their hopes raised only to be disappointed time and time again. The man some called the first black president from Hope, Arkansas, would change welfare as we had known it and institute a three strikes rule that sent some to prison for life for relatively minor crimes. One of the greatest times when black people felt optimistic about the possibility that their status and place in the American racialized social system would final change was with the election of President Barack

Obama. Unfortunately, evidence has shown that black people did not fare much better under the Obama Administration than other administrations. Some have defended President Obama and claimed that a hostile Republican majority kept him from doing more for black people, while others argue that he missed many opportunities to use the bully pulpit of the presidency to champion the rights of black people. He talked down to black people at an event sponsored by the NAACP, some have argued. He retreated when white people got upset when he said a white officer acted stupidly when he arrested famed scholar, Dr. Henry Louis Gates, a Harvard Professor, for allegedly breaking into his own house. President Obama simply held what was called a "Beer Summit," on the White House lawn. President Obama seemed to mourn with the nation at the killing of seventeen-year old Trayvon Martin in 2021, remarking that if he had a son he might look like Trayvon Martin, but did very little to draw attention to actively address the killing of black men, women, and children, especially by white police officers and ordinary white citizens.

Black people were hopeful that a Hillary Clinton presidency would bring about many of the substantive and structural changes they had longed for. It was Hillary Clinton who featured the Mothers of the Movement in her campaign. The Mothers of the Movement was a class that no parent wants to be in. The group was comprised of people like the mother of Trayvon Martin whose children were killed by white police officers or ordinary white citizens or while in police custody under suspicious circumstances. Millions of people, most of whom were white, voted instead to elect a real estate mogul who once took out a full-page ad in a national newspaper calling for the death penalty for a group of black and brown kids for allegedly assaulting a white woman in New York's Central Park, and who had a documented history of antiblack sentiments and who was accused of sexually assaulting more than one woman. For the next four years, black people and others endured President Trump's endorsement of white supremist groups and tolerance of antiblackness at all levels of society.

Given all that black America has endured, it is hard to imagine that many still have hope that their subordinate status in America will change. It is my contention that far too many black people were duped into believing that the gospel that is American civil religion applied to them when American civil religion was never intended to include nonwhite people.

American civil religion is a sociological concept that was introduced in 1967 by Robert Bellah. He argued that there existed a civil religion in America alongside other religions. Bellah (1967) argued that this civil religion, American civil religion was worthy of the same rigorous study as all other religions. In an effort to define American civil religion he analyzed presidential speeches. Bellah (1967) argued that the presidential inauguration was one of the most significant times in American civil religion, a high holy time, if you will. Bellah (1967) noted that in John F. Kennedy's inaugural address he mentioned God three times and that these references tell us what we need to know about civil religion in America. Bellah (1967) observed that Kennedy framed his remarks with comments about God. Kennedy invoked God twice at the beginning of his address and once at the end. Bellah (1967) found that this was a strategy used by other presidents on certain occasions but not usually to Congress when commenting on specific issues. Kennedy's remarks about God, Bellah (1967) claimed, reflect core values and commitments. The remarks pointed to a political realm with a religious dimension. American civil religion, for Bellah (1967), was characterized by a set of beliefs, symbols, and rituals.

Bellah (1967) also made the argument that it was during addresses such as the inaugural address that presidents, the high priests of American civil religion, offered religious legitimation for their authority. They espoused a collective and individual obligation to carry out God's will on earth. Bellah (1967) noted that before the Civil War, the Declaration of Independence and the Constitution were the most sacred scriptures in American civil religion. The Civil War, for Bellah (1967), introduced a new theme to American civil religion. The new theme was death. George Washington, according to Bellah (1967), was Moses in American civil religion and Lincoln was Jesus, or America's messiah. Bellah (1967) said that Memorial Day, for example, was a symbol of the death theme. He also argued that the theme for the 1960s was sacrifice, after the assassination of Kennedy. God, Bellah (1967) contended, was a central symbol in American civil religion.

Bellah (1967) outlined three important trials in American history. The first trial tackled the question of American independence (McDonald 2013). The second trial addressed slavery and the third trial contemplated reasonable action in a revolutionary war (McDonald 2013).

American civil religion, Bellah (1967) claimed, had its own prophets, martyrs, sacred events, sacred places, and solemn rituals and symbols. America's past, future, and present were in accordance with God's will and America was predestined to serve as a model for all nations, argued Bellah (1967). Bellah (1967) had some concerns about how American civil religion was being understood and used. He said, "it has been used and is being used today as a cloak for petty interests and ugly passions" (12).

Twenty years after the publication of Bellah's (1967) initial article on American civil religion, Mathisen (1989) provided some insights as to how, when, and why the concept fell out of favor with sociologists, religious scholars, and lay people. Mathisen (1989) wrote that the concept was popular in the 1980s but fell into decline. The period between 1967 and 1973 were described by Mathisen (1989) as the Golden Rules. The next four years represented the Golden Age. Between 1978 and 1982 interest in American civil religion plateaued, according to Mathisen (1989) and declined between 1983 and 1988. Mathisen (1989) argued that a lot of the critiques of Bellah's (1967) concept had to do with the definition, description, and interpretation of related historical events. Although American civil religion existed in three dimensions: historical reality, social construction, and academic discussion, it was not accepted by some as a significant religion and major sociology of religion journals simply stopped publishing articles on American civil religion in 1981 with few exceptions (Matisen 1989).

Hammond (1994) claimed that another challenge to Bellah's (1967) concept was that American civil religion was really just "idolatrous worship of the state" (Hammond 1994, 2). Another challenge was that some scholars viewed American civil religion as "simply a 'culture of religion'" (Hammond 1994, 2). Still others found that the "nation-centered religion" declined because of the civil rights movement and the Vietnam War (Hammond 1994, 3). Many scholars argued that American civil religion was hard to study using survey research and that the ontological status of American civil religion was unclear (Hammond 1994).

Whillock (1994) identified another set of issues with Bellah's (1967) concept. Whillock (1994) made the case that American civil religion suffered from competing value systems. Whillock (1994) identified common values and competing problems as one of the main limitations of Bellah's (1967) concept. American civil religion could best be understood as "a declaration of principles from competing groups seeking to define what America is and the values that should prevail," argued Whillock (1994, 375). In Whillock's (1994) evaluation, American civil religion was not a single belief system. Whillock (1994) even developed a typology to show the different types of belief systems. The typology included pilgrims, fundamentalists, pragmatists, and determinists (Whillock 1994). Pilgrims believed America was the Promised Land while fundamentalists focused on principles, such as patriotism, hard work, family, and respect for the law (Whillock 1994). Pragmatists, said Whillock (1994), emphasized the validity of statements and determinists held that individuals determined their future.

Compton (2019) was another scholar that addressed some problems with American civil religion. He said that Bellah (1967) miscalculated the role of religion in defining American civil religion. He did not adequately consider how religious groups would use American civil religion to mobilize for support or opposition to specific policy goals (Compton 2019). Furthermore, Compton (2019) also stated that Bellah (1967) was wrong to dismiss the role of Protestant, Jewish, and Catholic elites and institutions in connecting "abstract civil religious appeals to concreter policy programs" (Compton 2019, 3). Compton (2019) wanted to redefine American civil religion as religious nationalism and radical secularism. Religious nationalists want to link religion and politics and are not afraid to use violence. Compton (2019) said defined radical secularists call for the separation of religion and politics.

Fontanta (2010) was more optimistic about the continuing significance of American civil religion. Fontana (2010) argued that President Obama's candidacy and administration was evidence of the continuing significance of American civil religion. Like other presidents, President Obama's inauguration speech included religious and civil ideas (Fontanta 2010). Obama's version of American civil religion was said to be more cosmopolitan than previous presidents as he was far more inclusive than other holders of the office (Fontana 2010). Gedicks (2010), on the other hand, argued that American civil religion "now excludes too many Americans" (891). Religious pluralism, sectarian religious conservatism, and the image of the state as idolatry were also cited as contributing factors to Gedicks (2010) and others declaring themselves "a civil religion skeptic" (891).

It cannot be overlooked that Bellah (1967) expressed concern about the very concept he introduced. Despite publishing work critiquing it later in his career, he was, as Bortolini (2012) argued, a victim of his success. Bellah's (1967) idea became more important than him.

One of my main concerns with Bellah's (1967) original concept and much of the work that I have read that has followed it, with the exception of people like religious scholar, Charles Long (1999), is the lack of substantive engagement with issues of race, racism, and whiteness. Le (2020) was an exception to this trend in his attention to the colorblind rhetoric in the literature on American civil religion. Like me, he does not see this limitation as a justification for dismissing American civil religion altogether. In Le's (2020) work on monuments and American civil religion, he wanted to reconstruct the concept into what he calls "American national religion" (749). I disagree with Le (2020), but appreciate the emphasis that he placed on race, racism, and whiteness. Unlike for other scholars, for Le (2020), "the issue at hand is thus how race, religion, and nation are used to orchestrate social memory and advance certain futures" (768). Le (2020) wrote these words as he tried to make sense of American national memorialization through such things as monuments, in this case confederate monuments. Le (2020) clearly stated that he was bothered by the "failure to acknowledge the primacy of race in the religion of Americans as Americans" (768). Le (2020) referred to this failure as "descriptive blindness" (768). Le (2020) said that for the few scholars that have taken up the issue of race that "race is a secondary consideration" (769).

Race and racism have and continue to be among the most important determinants in America. Race and racism must be central in conversations, discourses, private practices, and public policies aimed at addressing racial inequities, which keep black people as a group at the lowest levels of America's racialized social structure.

Black people have historically accepted many myths about America, while at the same time remaining cautiously optimistic about the prospects of race relations actually changing in America in ways that would shift the racial caste system that has existed in American society for hundreds of years. At various times, some black people have embraced the myth of meritocracy or the idea that just putting forth one's best effort would lead to access to other myths, like the American dream. The pain and trauma enacted on black people who have endured generations, cycles, and peeks of progress (Bell 1992), was arguable best reflected in the writings of some of the nation's best black intellectual thinkers. Analyses of several well-known speeches or documents from these great black minds is illustrative of black people as whole feeling duped. These historical artifacts include "The Meaning of the Fourth of July to the Negro," by Frederick Douglas; by W. E. B. Du Bois's "Americanization," Martin Luther King, Jr.'s "I Have a Dream" and "Letter from the Birmingham Jail," James Baldwin's, "American Dream," and Toni Morrison's "The Slavebody and the Blackbody."

One July 5, 1851, abolitionist, Frederick Douglass, was invited to speak to a group of predominately white people on "The Meaning of the Fourth of July to the Negro." Douglass stated emphatically July was "your National Independence and your political freedom." He likened it to Passover. He talked about the hope he felt that the nation might change course with respect to its subordination of black people because it was still a relatively young nation. Douglass also addressed the impact of living in an unjust society. He said, "oppression makes a wise man mad." While Douglass acknowledged the audience's contribution to creating an independent nation he also shared the history of America with greater attention to the time in which he was delivering his address.

Douglass (1851) asked the listeners, "What have I, or those I represent, to do with your national independence? Are the great principles of political freedom and of natural justice embodied in that Declaration of Independence extended to us?" Douglass (1851), argued that "your high independence only reveals the immeasurable distance between us." Douglass (1851) wanted the audience to see the Fourth of July from the perspective of black men, women, and children held in physical bondage.

Douglass (1851) critiqued the hypocrisy and inconsistencies that dehumanized black people at the same time acknowledged them as rational beings as evidenced by the many laws controlling virtually every aspect of their lives. Douglass (1851) declared, "the hypocrisy of the nation must be exposed" (9). Speaking on behalf of slaves, Douglass (1851) asked, "What, to the American slave, is your Fourth of July? I answer: a day that reveals to him, more than all other days in the year, the gross injustice and cruelty to which he is the constant victim" (9). Douglass (1851) placed a figurative mirror up to America and encouraged them to see a different image looking back at them. Douglass (1851) wanted them to see what black people in America saw daily at the same time that many joined Douglass (1851) in hoping for change. Douglass (1851) added, "There is not a nation on the earth guilty of practices more shocking, and bloody than are the people of the United States" (9).

Douglass (1851) offered his own critique of religion and its support for the institution of slavery. He said, "but the church of this country is not only indifferent to the wrongs of slavery it actually takes sides with the oppressors" (13). The calls for political freedom simply did not apply to black people and were inconsistent with what members of the dominant group said they valued. Douglass (1851) made the argument that, "You boast of your love of liberty, your superior civilization, and your pure Christianity, while the whole political power of the names (as embodied in the two great political parties) is solemnly pledged to support and perpetuate the enslavement of millions of your countrymen" (15). Douglass (1851) ended his address where he started with hope. Ultimately, he said, "I do not despite of this country" (Douglass 1851, 17) but he cared enough about the status of black people, democracy, and the nation's potential to do better to critique it.

W. E. B. Du Bois's (1934), "A Negro Within a Nation," also reflected the tension between hope and despair that has characterized the lives of black people in America for generations. Du Bois described the 1930s as the most critical time in black life. Du Bois (1934) argued that the nation was ignoring calls "for elementary justice." Du Bois (1934) cited many of the issues facing black people today in his address almost a century ago. He cited unequal education, lynchings, employment discrimination, inadequate wages and low-prestige jobs (Du Bois 1934). Black people were limited in their employment opportunities to "common labor and domestic service" and black farmers were transformed to "landless tenants and peons."

Du Bois (1934) described how the myths that fueled the hopes of immigrants from Southern, Central, and Eastern Europe and black migrants from the South to the North resulted in black people being locked out of trade unions, restricted to poor neighborhoods, granted access only to poor housing, victims of discrimination and mob violence, and depression. Du Bois (1934) observed that since 1929, black workers were harmed more than other workers. Du Bois (1934) pointed to racial stratification that facilitated the assimilation of white ethnic groups and kept black people at the bottom and margins of American society. Du Bois (1934) was talking about the permanent subordination of black people back then. He said, "the loss has been greater and more permanent," for black workers than other workers (Du Bois 1934). Du Bois (1934) warned, "the colored people of America are coming to face that fact quite calmly that most white Americans do not like them." One glimmer of hope for black people might involve black people gaining economic and political power and developing a nation within a nation.

Dr. Martin Luther King, Jr.'s (1963), "I Have a Dream" is perhaps the most cited and (mis)quoted speech in modern American history. King (1963) was speaking about a number of issues, including jobs and freedom. He spoke on the theme of hope. In describing the Emancipation Proclamation, he saw it as a "light of hope to millions of Negro slaves" (223). King (1963) also signaled the feeling of betrayal that black people felt a century later given that black people were still not free. King (1963) cited segregation, discrimination, police brutality, voting limitations, and poverty as indicators. He said America had defaulted on a promissory note to black people and to the nation as a whole (King 1963).

One of best documents ever written about social justice and activism is without question, Dr. Martin Luther King, Jr.'s (1963), "Letter from the Birmingham Jail." One of the main messages was King's (1963) sentiment that he and other black people in America were duped into thinking that they could find friends among white Christians. The letter was a response to concerns from white clergy in Birmingham who were criticizing the demonstrations that were taking place (King 1963). King and other demonstrators were labeled extremists, law breakers, outsiders and anarchists, for trying to create a crisis and draw attention to the disrespectful and inhumane treatment black people endured (King 1963). King (1963) also drew upon the theme of hope. He stated, "our hopes have been blasted" by broken promises to remove racial signs in exchange for a moratorium on demonstrations (King 1963, 190). King (1963) masterfully captured the despair of black people then, before, and after the demonstrations. King (1963) observed that black people were "forever fighting a degenerating sense of 'nobodiness'" (192). King (1963) did, however, hold out hope that the freedom could be gained.

In James Baldwin's (1965), "American Dream," he also highlighted sentiments among black people that their hope in America was misplaced and that their social position would likely remain unchanged in perpetuity. Baldwin (1965) expressed that not only do American myths need to be debunked but that they were often created at the expense of black people. Baldwin (1965) said that for years black people have pledged allegiance to a flag that has not pledged allegiance to them. Baldwin (1965) addressed the many ways that black people were reminded "that you are a worthless human being." He added, as many have stated in more contemporary times that, "if it were white being people being murdered, the government would find some way of doing something about it." Baldwin (1965) like many other blacks thought leaders were calling into question whether black lives mattered long before the hashtag became popular.

How do we make sense of the permanent subordination of black people in America despite the existence of moments when black people and others seem hopeful that the nation will one day extend its creeds and core values to include black people? It is my contention that Derrick Bell's concept of racial realism provides the best explanatory power and also provides black people engaged in struggles to bring about transformative ways to find value in their fights. This book may be viewed as pessimistic by racial optimists, but it is best characterized as reflecting the racial realism that Derrick Bell outlined and that I argue is far too often underutilized in scholarly work and in social activism.

Chapter 1, "The Genius of Derrick Bell: Racial Realism," I discuss the dominant explanations for understanding the disappointment that black people have experienced throughout American history and continue to experience. I discuss Derrick Bell's concept of racial realism and explain why it provides the best explanation for understanding the dissatisfaction and disappointment that is the signature of the experiences of black people in America. I contrast Derrick Bell's racial realism with racial formation, colorblind racism, white racial frame, institutional racism, and Afro-pessimism.

In chapter 2, "Forty Acres and a Mule and Other Missed Opportunities," I show that one of the best examples of how black people in America were made promises that were not kept is historical and contemporary racial wealth inequality and black asset poverty. This chapter takes a deep dive into the origins of racial wealth inequality and the overrepresentation of black people among the asset poor and why black people have felt duped and disappointed. Attention is given to the roles of public policies and private practices. The chapter begins with the period of Reconstruction and includes the largest period of the mass accumulation of wealth in America and comments about the periods leading up to and after the Great Recession. I explore some noteworthy recommendations for addressing the racial wealth gap. Then, I address the importance of racial realism in understanding persistent racial wealth inequality between black and white people in America.

"The Myth of the Greatest Generation," chapter 3 examines the men and women who served in World War II and lived during this era who are often referred to the Greatest Generation. I explore what is meant by this phrase. Next, I debunk the myths associated with this idea, namely I question how this generation could be called the greatest given that antiblackness all but ruled the era. I discuss how black people were duped again and show why racial realism is an important tool for unpacking these important issues.

In chapter 4, "(Un) Civil Rights and Black Power," I contend that much has been written about the legislative successes of the civil rights movement and the effects of the Black Power movement. Despite the promises of both movements, black people continue to lag behind white people on a host of social and demographic outcomes. Again, black people were duped. Racial realism illuminates how the primary strategies of this era were actually ineffective and point to the perpetual subordination of black people in America. I provide insights that support Bell's claims.

In chapter 5, "Promises Unfulfilled: Black Lives Matter Chatter," I discuss #BlackLivesMatter—a popular hashtag that originated with the killing of Trayvon Martin in Sanford, Florida, by George Zimmerman. I discuss how it grew in popularity after the killing of George Floyd in Minneapolis, Minnesota, by several police officers. George Floyd's killing appeared to usher in a new or renewed interest in social justice issues. Colleges, universities, athletic teams, and corporations, among others, embraced the sentiments related to black lives matter. Racial realism helps us to understand, I argue, why many of the efforts were more symbolic than substantive and why black people again have felt an enormous sense of disappointment in the promise of America.

The book concludes with, "Racism, COVID-19, and Election 2020." I address the continuing significance of antiblackness. The conclusion also includes a discussion about how reactions to COVID-19 and the results of Election 2020 revealed a continued value gap between America as it is and America as it ought to be as well as the storming the U.S. Capitol on January 6, 2021, and responses to it. I call upon scholars to increase their engagement with Bell's racial realism and offer recommendations for restoring black people's faith in the promises of America.

*Chapter One*

# The Genius of Derrick Bell
## *Racial Realism*

Derrick Bell was a brilliant scholar and his commitment to illuminating the ongoing and permanent subordination of black people in America is beyond noteworthy. Bell (1992) was not only one of the most gifted scholars of his generation, but he was also among the bravest and unapologetic scholars. Bell (1992) cited empirical research to show that the condition of black people in America relative to other groups has not progressed as much as some scholars, elected officials, the mainstream media, and others would have us believe and described the subordination of black people as permanent—a finding that many find troubling.

Hope is an important American trope. One need only look at the political campaigns of former presidents, President Bill Clinton and President Barack Obama and in the famous rallying cry for Reverend Jesse Jackson. Reverend Jackson, himself a former presidential candidate and leader of the Rainbow Coalition, famously encouraged Americans to "Keep Hope Alive." President Clinton touted that he was from a place called Hope in Arkansas. President Obama led Americans in chants like, "Yes We Can!" and shared campaign material featuring his image and the word HOPE. Anthony Pinn, a scholar of African American religion, asks, "is hope a viable theological ethnical category?" (2020, 144). He also writes that "hope assumes reasonable response to material circumstance by embracing a mode of thinking and doing in line with the demands and restrictions of the historical mode of thinking and doing in line with the demands and restrictions of the historical moment" (Pinn 2020, 144). How might different ways of thinking about race assist in reconciling the seeming need for a collective imagination or "projection of what can be" (Pinn 2020, 146) with the realities of being black in America? This chapter includes a discussion about some of the dominant explanations for understanding the experiences of black people in America and the disappointment that black people have experienced throughout American history and continue to experience. The explanations include the writings of such black intellectual thinkers as W. E. B. Du Bois, E. Franklin Frazier, Franz Fanon, as well Marxism, class-based, internal colonialism, the politics of respectability, institutional racism, racial formation, colorblind racism, system racism, white racial frame, and Afro-Pessimism. I discuss Derrick Bell's (1992) concept of racial realism and explain why it provides the best explanation for understanding the dissatisfaction and disappointment that is the signature of the experiences of black people in America. I also share some of the ways Bell's (1992) concept is already being used to understanding the experiences of black people in education, the criminal justice system, residential segregation, and sports. I call upon race scholars in sociology, African American Studies, and other areas of study to expand their use of racial realism.

Du Bois was a dynamic scholar and he influenced many disciplines and areas of study, including sociology, African American Studies, and studies about race in general. As early as 1897, Du Bois wrote about the significance of race and the need for the conservation of the races. He argued that people make certain assumptions about black people in discussions about race. Du Bois (1897) felt such assumptions were wrong. Assumptions about black people related to their natural abilities, political aptitude, intelligence, and morality. In each case, it was widely assumed by the dominant racial group in America that black people were inferior to white people. Du Bois (1897) also made the argument that human beings are divided into races and the two most extreme types in the United States are black and white people. He called race relations significant to human history and asked a very important questions: "What is the real meaning of race; what has, in the past, been the law of race development and what lessons has the past history of race development to teach the rising Negro people?" (Du Bois 1897, 1).

Du Bois (1897) noted that historically the criteria for determining race were based on such characteristics as color, hair type, and head size. He observed that these and other biological characteristics varied widely between and within groups. Du Bois (1897) proclaimed that the history of the world was the history of groups. By groups, Du Bois (1897) was not referring to nations but races. For Du Bois (1897), race was the central thought of all history.

Race, for Du Bois (1897), could best be understood as common blood and language, common history, traditions, and working together for ideals of life. Globally, Du Bois (1897) described eight races: Slavs of Eastern Europe, Teutons of Middle Europe, Negroes of Africa and America, Semitic people of Western Asia and Northern Africa, the Hindoos of Central Asia, and the Mongolians of Eastern Asian. So-called minor races included American Indians or people indigenous to the Americas. Negroes were comprised of black people of mixed ancestry, Egyptians, Bantus, and Bushmen of Africa, according to Du Bois (1897).

For Du Bois (1897), physical differences were important in determining race, but he wrote that there were deeper differences. He described these as spiritual and psychical and contended that they transcended physical differences. Du Bois (1897) further argued the able people haven't given their full spiritual message to civilization. Du Bois (1897) thought that the best way to deliver the message was through the development of racial groups. For black people that meant the development of black literature, black art, black organizations, black colleges, and black businesses (Du Bois 1897). Du Bois (1897) laid out the framework for the establishment of a black academy, the American Negro Academy. The institution would be guided by a creed that included a commitment to making a unique contribution to civilization, maintaining racial identity, advocating for equality, respect for personal liberty and worth, and uplifting black people in America and Africa.

A few years later, *Philadelphia Negro* was not only one of Du Bois's (1899) most significant works but it was also one of the first empirical studies about race in America. In the classic study, Du Bois (1899) stressed the importance of studying black people empirically and not merely making assumptions about black people based upon stereotypes and myths. Du Bois (1899) used a multimethod approach and focused on the social conditions of the Seventh Ward in Philadelphia. Du Bois (1899) changed the way many people studied and thought about race. He showed empirically that while the problems of black people in this section of the city were diverse and that the people were diverse, it was white enforcement of racial discrimination that was to blame.

Du Bois (1903) wrote about the ongoing challenges that black people faced in America in *The Souls of Black Folk*. He asked a question that is still being asked today. How does it feel to be a problem? (Pinn 2020). He described how black people were often cut off from the world by a veil. The veil offered black people a second-sight or insider-outsider perspective. It is here that Du Bois (1903) introduces his classic concept of double-consciousness, which refers to black people having to look at themselves through the eyes of others. It includes a twoness: an American and a black person (Du Bois 1903).

While Du Bois (1899) understood race as a social construction and the social conditions of black people the result of racial discrimination at all levels of society, E. Franklin Frazier (1927) examined white people's treatment of black people through a psychological lens. In, "The Pathology of Racial Prejudice," Frazier (1927) argued that, "race prejudice is an acquired psychological reaction" (856). He went on to write that certain manifestations of race prejudice could best be understood as abnormal behavior. For Frazier (1927), there was a "dissociation of consciousness" for white people in their reactions to black people in any number of contexts (856).

Frazier (1927) outlined what he called the "Negro-complex" and defined it as "the system of ideas which most Southerners have respecting the Negro" (857). Frazier (1927) claimed the Negro-complex "has the same intense tone that characterizes insane complexes" (857). The intensity of the antiblack sentiments was so strong that statistical evidence to the contrary mattered little, if at all because, according to Frazier (1927), "the white man seizes myths and unfounded rumors to support his delusion about the Negro" (858). Frazier (1927) also showed how the process of rationalization, projections, and hallucinations were all part of what he called the pathology of racial prejudice. He wrote of "exaggerated antagonism" (Frazier 1927, 860), and the irony in the fear that many white people, especially in the South, expressed about black people. Frazier (1927) stated, "In the South, the white man is certainly a greater menace to the Negro's home than the latter is to his" (860). The process of rationalization, projections, and hallucinations have real consequences for black people. Taken together they made far too many white people "incapable of rendering just decisions when white and colored people are involved" (Frazier 1927, 862).

Despite Frazier's (1927) focus on the psychology of racial prejudice, Frazier (1949) argued in this later work that there was a relationship between race contacts and the social structure. Frazier (1949) urged sociologists to take the topic of race more seriously than in the past. He stated that sociologists were interested in how those who share a place and a culture carry out collective life. Frazier (1949) described the different schools of thoughts that existed for those who were engaged in studying racial contacts.

The normalist school, according to Frazier (1949), viewed society as "an aggregate of individuals and the key to an understanding of society is to be found in the study of the behavior of individuals as discrete units" (1). The realist or organic school, on the other hand, focused on "the social processes and the organized aspects of the collective life arising out of communication and interacting (Frazier 1949, 1). From Frazier's (1949) perspective, "studies of race relations have often been based upon individual reactions, without reference to the behavior of men as members of a social group" (1). Frazier (1949) urged scholars to understand racial contacts in the context of social relations. He dismissed the tendency on the part of sociologists to study black people as a social problem in American life. Viewing black people as a problem was rationalization of the social attitudes of the class in the white community from which sociologists were recruited (Frazier 1949). These views, for Frazier (1949), were based on previously published books and not on empirical studies. He denounced the general view that black people were an inferior race because of biology and/or social heredity and therefore could not assimilate and that miscegenation or "race mixing" was undesirable. Furthermore, Frazier (1949) pointed out that there was a perception that studies about black people did not have the same academic status as other sociological topics. Because black people had a relatively low status in America studies about black people were considered less significant (Frazier 1949).

Frazier (1949) acknowledged that at the time of his writing that more sociologists were taking race more seriously but continue to ignore systems of social control which the white community has used to maintain the racial status quo. Frazier (1949) highlighted the need for studies that focused not on attitudes but on the importance of the social structure and social contexts, namely topics like, spatial segregation, the family, the church, social norms, and values, social class, and urbanization.

Frazier (1949) observed that a caste and class school later emerged. This school focused on structural aspects of racial contacts but treated the caste concept as static (Frazier 1949). The caste and class school "ignored the dynamic aspects of race relations" (Frazier 1949, 3).

Franz Fanon (1952) offered insights to the study of race in *Black Skin, White Masks,* that took a similar approach to Frazier's (1927) work on the pathology of racial prejudice. Fanon (1952) used psychoanalysis in his attempt to understand black-white relations. Fanon (1952) stated "the white man is locked in his whiteness" (xiii). Fanon (1952) wanted to understand the being of the black man. He described two dimensions. One with fellow black people and the other with white people. Fanon (1952) said black men behave differently with another black than with a white man due in large part to the "white gaze" (90).

William Julius Wilson's book, *The Declining Significance of Race,* remains one of the most widely read, often cited, and controversial books in sociology. In the book, Wilson (1978) related racial issues to the economic and political arrangements of American society. He made the claim that changes in the system of production and in governmental polices changed black and white access to wealth, status, and prestige and it changed racial antagonisms. Wilson (1978) offered an explanation for changing race relations in America and discussed changes within the black population, specifically changes in the class structure. For example, Wilson (1978) argued that by the end of the twentieth century, the economic conditions for poor black people got worse and the economic conditions for the black middle class got better.

Three periods of American race relations were discussed in Wilson's (1978) book. The preindustrial period occurring during antebellum slavery. The industrial period began around 1875 and ended during the New Deal era. The modern industrial period occurred after World War II, according to Wilson (1978). Racial oppression was apparent in both the preindustrial and industrial eras in American race relations, wrote Wilson (1978). After World War II, the black middle class grew due to changes in civil rights legislation, the mass migration of black people from the South to the North and expanded economic opportunities for which they were prepared and then economic class became more important than race in determining the life chances of black people, argued Wilson (1978).

Joe Feagin was among the many scholars to take issue with Wilson's (1978) core contentions. Feagin (1991) disagreed with the characterization of the black middle class. He suggested Wilson (1978) and others underestimate the impact of racism on the black middle class (1994) and argued for the continuing significance of race. Feagin (1991, 1993) stated that the black middle class may face more overt racial discrimination because of their contacts with white people and their presence in white spaces, such as in schools and workplaces where white people were in the majority. Feagin (1991) described a discrimination continuum that included avoidance, rejection, verbal attacks, physical threats, and harassment by white police officers and physical threats by other whites. He outlined the many coping strategies that black people must employ in response to the various threats. These coping strategies include withdrawal, resigned acceptance, verbal confrontation, and physical confrontation (Feagin 1991). Feagin (1991) concluded that, "In spite of decades of civil rights legislation, black Americans have yet to attain the full promise of the American dream" (115).

Cheryl Harris wrote about whiteness as a form of property that empowers white people in the settings Feagin (1991, 1993) discussed. Specifically, Harris (1993) claimed that racial identity and property were interrelated concepts. Whiteness, for Harris (1993), is a form of racial identity and a form of property that is protected by law. This is evidenced by nonwhite people's attempts as claiming to be white or what scholars refer to as passing. Harris (1993) argued that passing has "a certain economic logic" (1713). Harris (1993) detailed the construction of race and the development of whiteness as property. Harris (1993) stated that racialization of identity and racial subordination provided the ideological basis for slavery, for example. Black people, during the enslavement period, were considered property. Only white people could possess land and the occupation of land validated property rights (Harris 1993). Said differently, there was a convergence of racial and legal status that led to "racial otherness," which in turn justified the lower status ascribed to black people (Harris 1993). The subordination of black people was codified by the law as early as the 1660s and created the dichotomies slave/free and black/white. Harris (1993) described the dual and contradictory character of slaves as property such as in the Three-Fifths Compromise, which counted black people as 60 percent of a person for the purpose of white political representation. The law served to legitimize whiteness as property (Harris 1993). Harris (1993) concluded with support for affirmative action to end the enduring oppression of black people.

Understanding whiteness as property informs challenges associated with the assimilation of black people. Assimilation has historically been used to understand the incorporation of white ethnic groups from Southern, Central, and Eastern Europe between 1880 and 1920 (Portes and Zhou 1993). Changes to U.S. immigration policy that took place in the mid-1960s, that led to the international migration of individuals from places like Latin America and Asian (Portes and Zhou 1993). Portes and Zhou (1993) examined second generation immigrants and found that race mattered for the newer immigrants in ways that it did not matter for older immigrants who were mostly white. Race made assimilation more difficult for new Americans and the extent to which some were incorporated into the broader society varied based upon the resources available to them, such as access to government programs and networks in ethnic communities.

Karyn Lacy (2007) contributed to research on race and the assimilation of black people in her book, *Blue Chip Black*. Lacy (2007) argued that black people strategically assimilate, such as in the case of black people living in various suburban contexts and their social class position. Middle class black people made efforts to keep one foot in the white world and one foot in the black world. They may live and work in majority white settings but in their private lives affiliate with majority black settings that were also middle class. I took issue with Lacy's (2007) argument in an article I published a few years after the release of Lacy's (2007) book where I contended that what Lacy (2007) described as strategic assimilation was better classified as a form of symbolic assimilation (Martin 2010).

Evelyn Higginbotham (1992) chronicled the history of black women in her discussion of race as a metalanguage. Higginbotham (1992) observed that feminist pay very little attention to race. Evelyn Nakano Glenn (1992) also conducted work on women's oppression and the role of race, especially where reproductive labor was concerned. Higginbotham (1992) wanted to center race and saw a need to define the construction and technologies of race. She exposed race as a metalanguage. Higginbotham (1992) understood race as sites of contestation. Higginbotham (1992) described "race as an unstable, shifting, and strategic reconstruction" (274).

In *Righteous Discontent*, Higginbotham (1993) told the story of black Baptist women and their efforts to control their images and destinies, while fighting for social justice. Higginbotham's (1993) book highlighted class differences within the black population and the commitment of black women to racial uplift between 1880 and 1920 that exposed shortcomings and opportunities for addressing antiblack sentiments.

One of the most progressive thinkers in sociology is Eduardo Bonilla-Silva. From the 1990s onward, he has made some conventional sociologists nervous and he has inspired many more critical sociologists and critical race scholars more broadly. In his work, "Rethinking Racism," Bonilla-Silva (1996) argued that many sociologists who claim to study race and racism have treated racism as if it needs no definition or theorizing. The assumption has been that racism is self-evident, charged Bonilla-Silva (1996). Historically, sociologists have regarded racism as ideological with a narrow focus on ideas. Even Marxists who consider the role of the means of production and class in understanding human history do not center race. Race is understood as a tool to divide social classes (Bonilla-Silva 1996). Bonilla-Silva (1996) offered criticism and praise for other perspectives on race.

Bonilla-Silva (1996) appreciated the work of institutionalists like Ture and Hamilton (1992), and their attention to the ways power and prejudice interact and facilitate institutionalized dominance at all levels of society. Likewise, Bonilla-Silva (1996) found merit in internal colonialism, which likened racial minorities to colonial subjects. Bonilla-Silva (1996), however, argued that "neither of these perspectives provides a rigorous conceptual framework that allows analysts to study the operation of racially stratified societies" (464).

Racial formation, introduced by Omi and Winant (1994), described the "'sociohistorical process by which racial categories are created, inhabited, transformed, and destroyed'" (Bonilla-Silva 1996, 466). Although racial formation represented an improvement over other treatments of race, according to Bonilla-Silva (1996), the perspective gave too much attention to certain actors, such as the far-right and liberals and did not emphasize the true character of racialized societies. Additionally, Bonilla-Silva (1996) found that racial formation focused excessively on ideological and cultural processes. Feagin and Elias (2013) also identified some issues with racial formation. The scholars contended that the perspective does not fully explain racial meanings and white racial framing. Moreover, Feagin and Elias (2013) did not think racial formation treated race as foundational to American society. Feagin and Elias (2013) suggested more attention to black counter-system analysts, such as W. E. B. Du Bois and Derrick Bell. Feagin and Elias (2013) instead call for treating race as "foundational, large-scale and inescapable hierarchical system of US racial oppression devised and maintained by whites and directed at people of color" (936).

Moon-Kie Jung and Yaejoon Kwon also critiqued racial formation in their effort to theorize about race in America. Jung and Kwon (2013) wanted to assert that the United States is not as a nation-state or an empire-state as was the case in racial formation but as a racial state where every state institution was a racial institution.

In asking sociologists and others to rethink racism, Bonilla-Silva (1996) offered a definition of racialized social systems. This term "refers to societies in which economic, political, social, and ideological levels are partially structured by the placement of actors in racial categories or races" (Bonilla-Silva

1996, 469). They all involve some form of ranking with those at the highest levels having the most access to economic benefits and political, power for instance. Taken together, racialized social relations and practices make up the racial structure of a society (Bonilla-Silva 1996). In order to rethink racism, Bonilla-Silva (1996) argued that racial phenomena must be understood as an expected outcome. The changing nature of racism should be understood as normal. Recognizing the existence of racialized social systems aids in our understanding of the existence of both overt and covert racial behavior. Moreover, Bonilla-Silva (1996) debunked the widely held myth that racism was somehow irrational and a sin of the past. Bonilla-Silva (1996) reminded scholars, and others, that racism is in the here and now. The distinctions between racial practices that reproduce racial inequality in contemporary times compared to in the Jim Crow era "(1) increasingly covert, (2) are embedded in normal operation of institutions, (3) avoid direct racial terminology, and (4) are invisible to most Whites" (Bonilla-Silva 1996, 476).

Bonilla-Silva (1999) addressed his critics in "The Essential Social Fact of Race." The criticisms included charges that he confounded race and ethnicity and reified race. Critics also disagreed with the significance Bonilla-Silva (1999) attributed to race. Bonilla-Silva (1999) characterized race as "a central principle of social organization" (899). Critics also rejected his claims that world-systematic racialization leads to the development of socially existing races (Bonilla-Silva 1999). Some scholars have raised objections about race and consciousness. Critics argued that race exists only if they are conscious of their existence and act as a collectivity (Bonilla-Silva 1999).

Charles Mills (1997) introduced the idea of the existence of a racial contract. He described a racial contract that was simultaneously political, moral, real, economical, and epistemological (Mills 1997). This "exploitation contract" was actual multiple contracts (Mills 1997, 10). Mills's (1997) racial contract "explains how society was created or crucially transformed, how the individuals in that society were reconstituted, how the state was established, and how a particular moral code and a certain moral psychology were brought into existence" (10). Mills (1994) showed how the racial contract could be formal or informal agreements between members of the white population in America. Under the racial contract, all whites were beneficiaries despite the fact that some whites may not be signatories (Mills 1997). One consequence of the racial contract is that nonwhite people become objects of the agreement.

Mills (2003) expanded his argument in his book chapter on white supremacy as a sociopolitical system. Mills (2003) observed that philosophers have largely ignored whiteness literature and argued that it was important for philosophers to understand whiteness as a social system. Mills (2003) added that white supremacy was a theoretical object. Mills (2003) concurred with other scholars that white supremacy is not a thing of the past and that power relations can have life beyond efforts to formally destroy them. Mills (2003) further argued that state and legal systems were not race-neutral. This is one dimension of white supremacy, according to Mills (2003). Mills (2003) identified several other dimensions of white supremacy, including economical, cultural, and metaphysical spheres. The culture sphere was characterized by the judgment that non-European cultures were inferior to European cultures. The economics sphere included the exploitation of black labor and the metaphysical sphere was characterized by racial inegalitarianism.

Scholars have also observed that not only has white supremacy survived over time but that a new form of racism emerged. This new racism has been described as colorblind racism (Thakore 2014). Bonilla-Silva (2002) is among the prominent scholars to unpack colorblind racism. He described the stylistic components of colorblind racism in "The Linguistics of Color Blind Racism." The components included white people avoiding the use of direct racial language and the engagement of semantic moves to find safe ways to talk about race (Bonilla-Silva 2002). The stylistic components of colorblind racism also included projection, the minimization of race, and what Bonilla-Silva (2002) could only describe as total incoherence. Bonilla-Silva (2002) said, "It is the task of progressive social scientists to expose color blindness, show the continuing significance of race, and wake-up color blind researchers to the color of the facts of race in contemporary United States" (63).

Afro-pessimism is among the more recent perspectives aimed at understanding race in America and the location of black people within American society and beyond. Jared Sexton is among the scholars associated with the emergence and development of Afro-pessimism. Sexton (2011) wrote about Afro-pessimism and the importance of terms like social death. Orlando Paterson introduced social death in his text on slavery and social death in the early 1980s (Chavez 2021). Paterson defined social death as "'permanent, violent domination of natally alienated and generally dishonored persons'" (Chavez 2021, 7). Indeed, Ernest Chavez (2021) says Afro-pessimism, at its core, is a reading of social death that engages antiblackness as foundational to civil society. "Social death might be thought of as another name for slavery and an attempt to think about what it comprises, and social life, then, another name for freedom and an attempt to think about what it entails" (Sexton 2011, 16). Afro-pessimism is "concerned here with the more specific emergence of freedom—as economic value, political category, legal right, cultural practice, lived experience—from the modern transformation of slavery into the convergence of the private property regime and the invention of racial blackness (which is to say the invention of antiblackness in the invention of whiteness, which cannot but become immediately a generalized nonblackness" (Sexton 2011, 17). For Sexton (2011), social death cannot be generalized to other groups as it is affixed to slavery. Afro-pessimism, according to Sexton (2011), is black optimism. Sexton (2011) reaches the conclusion that Afro-pessimism is black optimism when he asserts that "black social death is black social life. . . . The most radical negation of the antiblack world is the most radical affirmation of a blackened world" (37).

Anie Olaloku-Teriba (2018) offered a critique of Afro-pessimism. Olaloku-Teriba (2018) examined the theoretical limitations of antiblackness as an analysis of racialized oppression drawing from people like Frantz Fanon and Steve Biko, the South African activist and black intellectual thinker. Olaloku-Teriba (2018) wanted to move the literature from an overreliance on relational social theory to identarian essentialism. Olaloku-Teriba (2018) argued that there was a tendency among Afro-pessimists and some other race scholars to universalize analysis of racial categories with unanswered questions about blackness. What remains unknown, according to Olaloku-Teriba (2018) were questions about how to define blackness and who may possess blackness. One of the challenges Olaloku-Teriba (2018) identified in their work was how Afro-pessimism has both shaped definitions about blackness and also been shaped by definitions of blackness. Afro-pessimism suffers from a relatively narrow definition of blackness that is an Americanization of the concept of blackness, which may not be useful for understanding blackness in other contexts (Olaloku-Teriba 2018).

## DERRICK BELL'S RACIAL REALISM

Derrick Bell was not only a great legal scholar, but he also worked previously for the US Department of Justice and on behalf of the National Association for the Advancement of Colored People (NAACP) alongside legal giants like Justice Thurgood Marshall on a host of civil rights cases. Despite this rich legacy of using the courts to fight racial injustices, Bell (1992) concluded that racial equality was an unrealistic goal. For example, Bell (1992) was involved in school desegregation cases but ultimately concluded that some of the decisions were only symbolic. In the case of *Brown*, Bell (2004) argued that the once landmark case had become irrelevant and that the process by which it was reached followed a familiar pattern whereby black interests are considered only when interest converges with white policymakers. The convergence is more important than black misery (Bell 2004). Secondly, when white policymakers feel the remedy is a threat to white supremacy than support for it ends (Bell 2004). Finally, black people are always vulnerable targets to be sacrificed (Bell 2014). Far too frequently, black people become part of "silent covenants" or "agreements based on interest convergence and those sacrificing black rights in order to settle differences between contending white groups" (Bell 2014, 26). Bell (1992) introduced racial realism as a challenge to coping with the aforementioned pattern and as a challenge to the very idea of racial inequality.

Bell (1992) defined racial realism as "a legal and social mechanism on which blacks can rely to have their voice and outrage heard" (364). He likened racial realism to legal realism and the attempts on the part of legal realists to change jurisprudent thought (Bell 1992). He wrote that in the early part of the twentieth-century legal realists challenged the classical structure of law. They did not see the law as simply common law rules that when applied appropriately would lead to results that were right and just. In essence, legal realists challenged the ridged ways of the past (Bell 1992). Legal realists applied a critical lens and attitude toward the law, while formalists focused instead on claims that the law was logical, self-evident, objective, and consistent (Bell 1992). Legal realists contended that the law was changing, subjective, and impacted by value-laden and personal beliefs (Bell 1992). Legal realists stressed "the function of law" not "the abstract conceptualization of it" (Bell 1992, 366). The lack of critical perspective about the law covered up "the reality of economic and political power" (Bell 1992, 368).

Bell (1992) cited the historic *Bakke* case as evidence of how racism can provide a reason for a judge to rely on a particular premise over some other premise when incompatible claims are present. Bakke, a case involving admissions to medical school and considerations of race that had a negative effect on affirmative action initiatives, relied on the Fourteenth Amendment and ignored important social questions about race, claimed Bell (1992). Bell (1992) said the court failed to consider statistical evidence, employ flexible reasoning, or take into account historical patterns. At the very least, argued Bell (1992), the court should have considered the poor quality of schools in areas that are majority black, the absence of professional black role models, and the use of discriminatory standardized tests. Instead, the judges relied on abstract concepts such as equality to hide their policy choices and value judgements (Bell 1992).

Bell (1992) described what he called "peeks of progress," or "short-lived victories that slide into irrelevance as racial patterns adapt in ways that maintain white dominance" (373). Bell (1992) said, racial realism "requires us to acknowledge the permanence of our subordinate status" (373–374). He added that doing so "enables us to avoid despair and frees us to imagine and implement racial strategies that can bring fulfillment and even triumph" (Bell 1992, 374).

William Abrams disagreed with Bell's (1992) claims that blacks were forever destined to hold the lowest possible position in society. Abrams described racial realism as "weary despair" (Abrams 1992, 517). Abrams (1992) agreed with Bell (1992) that there was a need to rethink strategies around civil rights issues but did not see racial realism as one of them. Racial realism, for Abrams (1992), could best be understood as "unconditional surrender" (Abrams 1992, 518). Abrams (1992) was also not pleased that Bell (1992) did not offer any alternate solutions or direction for civil rights advocates. Abrams (1992), further disputed Bell's (1992) argument about evidence dating back hundreds of years to support his argument that racial equality was not possible. Abrams (1992) wrote, "That more than 300 years has passed since African Americans began their struggle for racial justice and equality is not evidence that blacks will never gain justice and equality in the United States," but does not argue with the accuracy of Bell's (1992) initial argument, which volumes of data support.

George Taylor (2004) wanted to address the apparent contradiction in Bell's (1992) comments that the subordination of black people was permanent but that there was also value in struggle. Taylor (2004) and other scholars have suggested that Bell's (1992) assertion was religious (Stefancic 2018). Taylor (2004) thought Bell's (1992) paradox should be considered through the lens of theory and not social science. Taylor (2004) cited Niebuhr theory and its emphasis on the possibility of action in the face of sin and called for a social realism. Charles Long (1986) provided a better explanation as to how racial realism could be religious in his book, *Significations.* Long defined religion as an orientation. It is a way that people come to understand their place in the world (Finley et al. 2018; Gray, Finley, and Martin 2019). Stephen Finley, Biko Gray, and I argued that whiteness is religious in our edited volume, *The Religion of Whiteness,* and we drew a great deal of inspiration from Long's classic work (Finley et al. 2020).

Gregory Park sought to improve upon Bell's (1992) concept of racial realism with what he described as a critical race realism. Park (2008) defined critical race realism as a synthesis of critical race theory, public policy, and empirical social science. Park (2008) showed an appreciation for each, including Bell's (1992) work to develop a more comprehensive framework that consisted of a deconstructive element and a constructive element. The deconstructive element which would include a race-based assessment of the law and legal institutions. The constructive element would lead to a more progressive policy agenda that centered race (Park 2008).

Critiques of racial realism notwithstanding, Bell (1992) left a legacy that lives on but should be more expansive. Francisco Valdes (2014) detailed some of Bell's (1992) contributions to society and his legacies. Valdes (2014) credited Bell (1992) with connecting traditional storytelling with legal scholarship and using critical narrative to generate new knowledge. Valdes (2014) claimed Bell made masterful use of parables over the course of his work and life. Bell also centered race and illuminated the existence and consequences of white supremacy (Valdes 2014). Bell's legacies include the connections he made between civil rights legislation and court decisions and interest convergence. Another legacy of Derrick Bell was the idea that service to a just cause was praiseworthy. Freedom requires more than one actor and fighting to change the racial status quo involves risks. Additionally, Bell's life work served as a reminder that resistance was important even in the midst of despair. Bell's legacy also includes studies that build upon his work and introduce related concepts, including educational and penal realism, segratory realism, and racial realism.

## EDUCATIONAL AND PENAL REALISM

Kenneth Fasching Varner and his colleagues draw upon Bell's (1992) work on racial realism and Feagin's (2013) white racial frame to develop a theory of educational and penal realism in their 2017 article published in *Equity & Excellence in Education*. The scholars address racial disparities in education and in prisons as normal outcomes of a racialized social structure. They highlight efforts to disenfranchise black people for the benefit of the dominant racial group in America and link the efforts to economic principles of the market. They track the economic interests of the prison industrial complex alongside the educational reform industrial complex. The former claims to address crime and related reforms and the latter school failures. The aim of the scholars is to change the conversation about schools and prisons as a means of "empowering those interested in critically engaging issues of racism that permeate U.S. orientations to education and justice" (Fasching Varner et al. 2014, 410). The scholars outline seven tenets:

1. There is no crisis in schools or prisons—each institution is functioning per their design and the demands of society (Fasching Varner et al. 2014, 421).
2. Neither schools nor prisons will ever represent, serve, or address the interests of the most marginalized and underrepresented of society but they will do so for those from dominant and overrepresented fractions of society (Fasching Varner et al. 2014, 421).
3. Economic imperatives are the central driving force in decisions to sort and separate the marginalized from the oppressors both in education and correction (Fasching Varner et al. 2014, 421).
4. All sectors in the system whether well intended or not, both contribute to and benefit from educational and correctional oppression—desires to serve in activist roles have limits, through convergence with personal economic interests (Fasching Varner et al. 2014, 423).
5. Because personal and private interests allow for human sacrifice, populations of color and those of poor socioeconomic standing will continue

to be offered up in service of the historically and contemporarily overrepresented particularly through schooling and correction efforts (Fasching Varner et al. 2014, 423).
6. Equality is a ruse aimed at distracting the populous. Even if equality were achievable, the term suggests that the dominant group is still the valued group furthering assimilationist principles geared toward the privileged (Fasching Varner et al. 2014, 424).
7. Equity, consequently, is the only potential course of action that could counterbalance the racist underpinning of both educational and correctional structures (Fasching Varner et al. 2014, 424).

Kenneth Fasching Varner and I also used Bell's (1992) racial realism and white racial frame to explain enduring residential segregation amid growing racial and ethnic diversity in America and why initiatives aimed at addressing residential segregation have been largely unsuccessful. We argued that "residential segregation is no accident but is one of a host of expected outcomes of a racially stratified system that was in plan concurrent with the founding of the 'democracy' of the United States" (Fasching Varner and Martin 2017, 1). We offered several "working tenets of 'segregatory realism,' a realism that may address the segregation across sectors, especially housing . . . and that might serve thoughts interested in conceptualizing and renegotiating the ways in which reform is approached" (Fasching Varner and Martin 2017, 7). We argued that the following tenets were foundational to answering questions about the very idea of democracy.

The first tenet holds that residential segregation was not the result of personal preferences but was an outcome of an unjust racial social system. The second tenet contented that space serves the interests of the dominant racial group in America. The next tenet addressed the role of economic interests in dictating the marginalization of black people and other people of color in housing. The fourth tenet described how black bodies were offered up in sacrifice to the economic interests of the dominant racial group. The fifth and sixth tenets contrast equality and equity and warns against calls for black people, for example, to assimilate into the dominant culture as a means for achieving greater parity in housing and promotes instead, equity, which "creates solutions that intentionally engage differences to remedy past treatment. Any solution forward cannot simply involve walking away from hundreds of years of oppression based on the simplistic notion of equality. Equity is unapologetic in working to divert and reinvest financial, emotional, and collective resources, in disproportion, to counteract what had already been in place" (Fasching Varner and Martin 2017, 8).

## RACE, RELIGION, AND AMERICAN CIVIL RELIGION

As mentioned previously, Bell's (1992) racial realism concept may be understood as religious. In this section of the chapter, I show religion is related to racial realism using the backdrop of sports, namely responses to black athletes protesting against racial injustice during the performance of their sport. In addition to engaging with Bell's (1992) work, I am also in conversation with an oft-neglected sociological concept, American civil religion.

Sociologist, Robert Bellah, introduced the concept of American civil religion in the late 1960s. Bellah (1967) makes the argument that American civil religion exists alongside other religions and should be treated as seriously and with the same care. Bellah (1967) focused on the historical documents, such as the Declaration of Independence, the U.S. Constitution, and presidential addresses, and why God is mentioned, the way God is mentioned, and the associated meanings. Bellah (1967) noted America's obligation, given the messages communicated in these important texts, to carry out God's will on earth. Bellah (1967) further outlined the main elements of civil religion more broadly and then discusses what he views at key trials. The key trials Bellah (1967) mentioned were independence, full institutionalization of democracy, and responsible action in a revolutionary world. These trials coincided with important times in American history, including the American Revolution, the Civil War, and the modern-day civil rights movement.

For Bellah (1967) civil religions acknowledge God, the life to come, rewards of virtue and negative sanctions for wrongdoings, and the exclusion of religious intolerance. American civil religion, I argue, represents a departure from other civil religions in that Judeo-Christianity as practiced by a majority of white Americans does not exclude religious intolerance. There are many examples of religious intolerance particularly aimed at Muslims both before and after the attacks on September 11, 2001 (Curtis 2017, 2018, 2020). Bellah (1967) sees Christianity and American civil religion as separate. He cautioned that American civil religion was not the worship of the American nation but an understanding of the American experience in light of ultimate and universal reality. I contend the two are constitutive. Moreover, while Bellah (1967) did not significantly address the role of race in American civil religion, one cannot separate the intersections of race, white Judeo-Christianity, and American civil religion.

Charles Long's work brilliantly explains the connections. Long (1986) wrote, "American religion is usually understood as the religion of European immigrants transplanted into the American soil" (161). American religion often excludes black people and other nonwhites. Long added that American civil religion essentially does the same thing and sees the language in the

Declaration of Independence and the Constitution differently than Bellah (1967), for example. Long (1986) wrote, "the religious vision stemming from this orientation differs from the revealed religion, Christianity, for the revealed religion offers salvation to all human beings regardless of circumstances, whereas, in civil religion, salvation is seen within the context of belonging to the American national community" (161). American means European Christian immigrants and their descendants and religion means Christianity and its institutions to the exclusion of American Indians and black people and the black, American aborigines, Asian Americans and other religions (Long 1986). In short, American civil religion is "serving to enhance, justify, and render sacred the history of European immigrants in this land" (Long 1986, 162). Long argued, "The religion of the American people centers around the telling and retelling of the mighty deeds of the white conquerors. This story hides the true experience of Americans from their very eyes. The invisibility of Indians and blacks is matched by a void or a deeper invisibility within the consciousness of white Americans" (163). W. E. B. Du Bois's (1921) commented about the religion of whiteness in *Darkwater* describe it as personal, modern, and claims of ownership of the earth.

Since Long's (1986) work, other scholars have written about whiteness and the dangerous consequences of not seeing the humanity of black people (Efird and Lightfoot 2020, Finley, Gray, and Martin Forthcoming, McDonald 2005, 2012, Perkinson 2004, Winddance and Gallagher 2008, Yancy 2000, 2005). Charles Mills (1997), for example, described whiteness or white supremacy as a political system that "is the background against which other systems, which we *are* to see as political are highlighted" (2). Sara Ahmed (2007) said whiteness is an "ongoing and unfinished history" (149). Whiteness is real. It is a form of orientation, argued Ahmed (2007). Abdul-Rauf's refusal to stand in a "dignified" posture and his claim that the American flag could be interpreted as a symbol of oppression runs counter to the dominant narrative.

White reactions to the overrepresentation of black people among COVID-19 deaths and the killing of George Floyd are two recent examples highlighting the invisibility within the consciousness of white Americans that Long describes (1986). In many cities across the country more than 70 percent of COVID-19 related deaths were black deaths. People from President Trump on down the political ladder seemed baffled by the overrepresentation of black people among the dead as if they were totally oblivious to the longstanding racial disparities in the health care system and in virtually every other area of America society that makes black people particularly vulnerable, including during pandemics and economic downturns. The use of excessive force by police and fatal shootings of black people by ordinary white citizens provides some of the best evidence of the invisibility of black people within the consciousness of white Americans. From the anti-lynching campaigns championed by Fannie Lou Hamer to the anti-police brutality comments by Dr. Martin Luther King to the killing of George Floyd black people have been sounding the alarm about the many ways in which they were dehumanized and terrorized (King 1963, Martin 2019). Even for those white individuals and institutions issuing statements and joining demonstrations following the killing of George Floyd the gap between what they say they support and the ways they have behaved in the past and continue to behave are telling. Abdul-Rauf's protest was part of the longstanding tradition of trying to raise the consciousness of white Americans on issues related to black suffering and black deaths.

The backlash Abdul-Rauf faced was based upon his blackness, his religion, and his critique of American society and its treatment of nonwhite people within its borders and across the globe. The reactions to his protests reflect two functions of American civil religion. Grace Kao and Jerome Copulsky (2007) wrote about American civil religion and the Pledge of Allegiance. In their analysis, they describe four functions of American civil religion. The four functions are preservationists, pluralist, priestly, and prophetic. I wish to focus on priestly and the prophetic in this chapter. Abdul-Rauf's protests are reflective of the prophetic function of American civil religion (Copulsky 2018). The prophetic function, according to Kao and Copulsky (2007) advocates for civil rights, which is what Abdul-Rauf hoped to accomplish. The priestly function legitimizes the state, institutions, and policies. It seeks to wed God and country. The playing of the national anthem is then best understood as a "religious proclamation" (127), "secular ritual" (129), and "ceremonial deism" (130). White responses to Abdul-Rauf's efforts to offer a critique of American society are rooted in the priestly function. Thus, Abdul-Rauf is considered by those embracing the priestly function of American civil religion as ungrateful and unappreciative of all that American has given him and is invited by some white fans to leave the country of his birth. His actions were considered an affront to the way in which members of the dominant group in America understand their place in the world. Social institutions, such as sports may be understood as "orientation devices" (Ahmed 2007, 157). Within sports and other institutions "recruitment functions as a technology for the reproduction of whiteness" (Ahmed 2007, 157). So, white fans think because they recruited and supported "Chris Jackson" who became Mahmoud Abdul-Rauf that they were somehow deceived because he no longer represented the kind of black athlete they could "support." Abdul-Rauf's protest thrust him into the collection of bodies that "stand out when they are out of place" (Ahmed 2007, 159). Finley and Martin (2017) put it this way,

> There is much that is regarded as sacred in the religion of whiteness. Values such as justice, freedom, fairness, and democracy are considered sacred for white

people in America in so far as they apply to individuals with membership in the dominant racial group. The apparent gap between what America says it values and how it actually treats black people and other people of color is not American society operating in a way that is contradictory as some have suggested; rather it is the religion of whiteness at work which considers said values as sacred and views whiteness's sin as blackness. The inability to indict white people, e.g., white police officers responsible for killing unarmed black men and boys, despite claims that anyone can indict a ham sandwich, is considered justice. Proclaiming black lives matter is viewed as sacrilegious (186) and this is the racial injustice informing Abdul-Rauf's decision not to join in a ritual involving symbols with meanings are not necessarily shared by all.

## RELIGIOUS REALISM

Abdul-Rauf was of course not the last athlete to use his high-profile position to draw attention to America's many shortcomings and because of an unwillingness on the part of many with membership in the dominant group, especially those with a strong adherence to American civil religion, he will not be the last. The experiences of Colin Kaepernick are well known. Like Abdul-Rauf, Kaepernick experienced a great deal of backlash. While Abdul-Rauf was traded and rendered relatively invisible by his new team and the National Basketball Association in general, he was able to continue his career and remains an active elite basketball player today (Brockell 2019, Washington 2016). Kaepernick, on the other hand, was not signed to any teams once he became a "free agent." Kaepernick became a free agent shortly after he started the anthem protests and others from around the sports world joined him. Despite an eventual tryout that caused some Kaepernick supporters to question the sincerity of the event, he remains unsigned today. Moreover, after the killing of George Floyd, Roger Godell, Commissioner of the NFL, issued a statement on behalf of the league where he apologized for not listening to the players about what they were actually protesting but he made no mention of Kaepernick or their mistreatment of him, nor did they offer Kaepernick his rightful place on any team's roster. While the individual stories may change over time, from the days of Ali, Smith, Carlos, Abdul-Rauf, to Kaepernick, what remains the same is the significance of the religion of whiteness and American civil religion.

How might we explain the lack of sustained racial progress in sports and in American society despite the personal and collective sacrifices of some elite athletes and many members of the black community? Legal scholar, Derrick Bell (1992), would characterize events like the apology from the NFL and even the interracial protesting following the killing of George Floyd as peaks of progress. Bell (1992) offered a strategy for coming to terms with the lack of long-term progress with respect to race relations in America. He proclaimed, "racial equality is in fact, not a realistic goal" and describes America as "perilously racist" (Bell 1992, 363). Bell (1992) viewed racial realism as a "challenge to the principle of racial equality" (Bell 1992, 364). Racial realism calls for an acknowledgment of the permanence of the subordinate status of black people in America. In so doing, black people can "avoid despair" and free black people "to imagine and implement racial strategies that can bring fulfillment and even triumph" (Bell 1992, 374). Bell (1992) warned that "contemporary color barriers are less visible but neither less real nor less oppressive" (374).

Kenneth Fasching-Varner and his colleagues (2014) drew inspiration from Bell's (1992) work on racial realism and introduced educational and penal realism. The concepts focused on race and the school-to-prison pipeline and residential segregation, respectively. I published an article with Fasching-Varner where we introduced segregatory realism (Martin and Fasching-Varner 2017). Here we applied the concept of racial realism to residential segregation. In this book chapter, I introduce religious realism, which is *to acknowledge the permanence of both whiteness as religious and the subordinate status of black athletes and other black people in the sport industrial complex.* The following six tenets should inform conversations about where we go from here regarding race, religion, and sports.

First, racial disparities exist in sports and in society by design. While some people see sports as one of the few places in society where the playing field is level, there are many examples that this is not the case. One need only look at how black and white athletes are represented differently in the media or compare the percentages of black players in the National Football League compared to the number of black majority team owners or even the number of coaches. American society is structured in such a way that these observed racial differences represent expected outcomes and do not occur purely by chance.

Second, policies aimed at addressing racial disparities in sports and in society often exacerbate disparities and seldom go far enough. Far too often American sports leagues, corporations, and communities attempt to address persistent racial disparities through the creation of seemingly race-neutral policies and practices. One cannot address racism in sports without adequately taking account of race. Hence, it means little in the grand scheme of things to revise policies about how one should conduct themselves during the playing of the national anthem while doing little if anything to make whole the former player impacted most by the league's actions. Additionally, the recent changes to the Rooney Rule requiring now two external minority candidates for head coaching positions appears promising but does not account for the ongoing unequal treatment black coaches receive when compared with white coaches. Black coaches are often terminated more quickly and held to different standards than white coaches across leagues. Hiring and retaining black coaches must be a priority and creating an environment that is welcoming to black coaches is imperative but not likely.

Third, the religion of whiteness is the catalyst for ongoing racial inequalities in sports and other American social institutions. So much of what happens at every level of sports in America is driven by concerns about how white people will respond and the economic implications of those responses. Because whiteness is an orientation, threats to it are often met with a great deal of fervor that can best be described as religious. Decision-makers in all parts of the sports industrial complex will gladly "allow for human sacrifice; populations of color and those of poor-socioeconomic standing, consequently, are continually offered up in service to benefit the economic interests of Whites" (Martin and Fasching-Varner 2017, 8). This is particularly true for black athletes, black people throughout the sports industrial complex, and black people as a whole.

Fourth, persistent racial inequality in sports creates a misery loop for black people in the U.S., the impact of which may be felt in other areas of social life. Scholars have written about racial battle fatigue and the health impacts associated with living with racism. Black athletes and other black people associated with sports in America live under *the smog of terror* as Henrika McCoy (2020) describes it, or the state of intense or overwhelming fear. They live with the fear that anything they say or do that challenges whiteness may result in any number of consequences from the loss of one's career, violence, or threats of violence. This is in addition to the terror black athletes and other black people in the world of sports experience in the wake of threats to, and the killing of, black people for just being (McCoy 2020).

Fifth, protests by black athletes will always be seen as a threat to the religion of whiteness. When black athletes protest against injustices in America, they are debunking the myth that the country has long served as a liberator focusing instead on the many ways America has been the oppressor. The religion of whiteness entails members of the dominant group seeing themselves as virtuous, godly, and in some cases, god-like (Finley and Gray 2015). Thus, protests by black athletes must not only be rejected but following such protests, black athletes will be encouraged to adopt "assimilationist principles geared toward" white decision-makers and the predominately white fan base.

Six, black athletes should continue to develop strategies to bring fulfillment and triumph in the sports industrial complex, and the society-at-large without an expectation of equality or equity. For years black athletes have used their positions to draw attention to racial injustices within their sport and in the broader society. In addition to the names already mentioned, we could add the names of people like, Curt Flood, who likened the lack of free agency to slavery or to Jackie Robinson who was critical of Major League Baseball for the lack of black representation on coaching staffs and front offices (Martin 2014, 2019). Current and former elite athletes like LeBron James and Magic Johnson should be commended for their investments into black school children and black businesses, for example, and for speaking out about racial inequalities. Black athletes and black people as a whole should not despair when despite their efforts (and the efforts of others) racial differences on a host of outcomes persist.

Mahmoud Abdul-Rauf's challenge to America's self-image in the 1990s and the reactions from the largely white fan base have not received very much scholarly attention and although the scant scholarly treatments offer important insights they are also limited in some ways, namely the underestimation of antiblack sentiments in sports and in the country. To address this limitation, I discussed the relationship between race, racism, and sport. I examined American civil religion and then showed how Abdul-Rauf's protest reflected American civil religion's prophetic function. Additionally, I addressed how the negative reactions to Abdul-Rauf's stance by mostly white fans reflected the priestly function. I linked American civil religion to whiteness and the religion of whiteness. Lastly, I introduced religious realism as a way of moving conversations forward about racism in sports and in the U.S. in general with six important tenets.

In Dr. Martin Luther King's (1963) "Letter from the Birmingham Jail," he responded to criticisms from a group of mainly white clergy about his involvement in direct actions in Birmingham, Alabama. In one part of King's (1963) response letter he stated, "You warmly commended the Birmingham police force for keeping 'order' and 'preventing violence.'" He added, "I cannot join you in your praise of the Birmingham police department." Then, King (1963) proclaimed, "I wish you had commended the Negro sit inners and demonstrators of Birmingham for their sublime courage, their willingness to suffer and their amazing discipline in the midst of great provocation."

Mahmoud Abdul-Rauf and other activist black athletes show great courage and endure much suffering and are the real heroes, according to King (1963). Black athletes are not immune from the impacts of racism. When black athletes speak truth to power, they face resistance, especially from white fans and white decision-makers throughout the sports industrial complex. The religious fervor with which white people respond to black athletes deemed out of place is worthy of further serious scholarly inquiry.

In this chapter I examined the dominant explanations of race in America, specifically, the subordination of black people. I reviewed the arguments laid out in Bell's (1992) introduction of racial realism. I discussed his legacy from the perspective of other scholars and some of my own work and the work of my colleagues that were inspired by Bell's (1992) willingness to be unapologetic in his discussion of the futility of focusing on racial inequality, acknowledge the permanent subordination of black people in America, and his call to continue in the struggle despite the expected outcome. In the next chapter, I argue that one of the best examples how black people in America were made promises that were not realized is historical and contemporary racial wealth inequality and black asset poverty. I take a deep dive into the origins of racial wealth inequality and the overrepresentation of black people among the asset poor and why black people have felt duped and disappointed. Attention is given to the roles of public policies and private practices. The chapter focuses on the period of Reconstruction through the World Wars. I also discuss the importance of racial realism in understanding persistent racial wealth inequality and black asset inequality in more contemporary times.

*Chapter Two*

# Forty Acres and a Mule and Other Missed Opportunities

One of the best examples of how black people in America were made promises that were not realized is historical and contemporary racial wealth inequality and black asset poverty. This chapter takes a deep dive into the origins of racial wealth inequality and the overrepresentation of black people among the asset poor and why black people have felt duped and disappointed. Attention is given to the roles of public policies and private practices. The chapter focuses on the period of Reconstruction through the World Wars. I also discuss the importance of racial realism in understanding persistent racial wealth inequality and black asset inequality.

## RACIAL WEALTH INEQUALITY IN AMERICA

Wealth and income are two distinct but related concepts. Wealth includes all of an individual's or a household's assets minus liabilities. Income can best be understood as earnings from employment or as wages. Melvin Oliver and Thomas Shapiro (1995) authors of the classic book, *Black Wealth White Wealth*, wrote one of the definitive works on the linkages between race and wealth. Oliver and Shapiro (1995) defined wealth as "a particularly important indicator of individual and family access to life chances" (710). Unlike income, wealth may be "used to create opportunities, secure a desired stature and standard of living, or pass class status along to one's children" (710). Wealth is "more encompassing than is income and education, and closer in meaning and theoretical significance to our traditional notions of economic well-being" (710). When we look at wealth, according to Oliver and Shapiro (1995), it "helps solve the riddle of seeming black progress alongside economic deterioration" (710). Focusing on racial wealth inequality challenges how we understand social justice and race in America, argued Oliver and

Shapiro (1995). "Wealth reveals a particular network of social relations and a set of social circumstances that convey a unique constellation of meanings pertinent to race in America" (711).

W. E. B. Du Bois, an American sociologists, examined census records for 1890 and 1900 in an attempt to determine the value of black property in North Carolina, Virginia, and Georgia. In 1890, about 19 percent of black families owned their homes or farms (Du Bois 1910). In 1900, the number rose to about 22 percent (Du Bois 1910). About 188,000 farms in the United States were owned by black people. Close to twelve million acres were owned by black people, according to Du Bois's (1910) analyses. The farm property was worth about $175 million in 1900 and in 1899 black people owned more than $50 of farm products (Du Bois 1910).

In North Carolina, the assessed value of black property increased by 124 percent between 1900 and 1908. In Virginia it increased by 62 percent between 1900 and 1908. Georgia saw a nearly 92 percent increase in black property between 1900 and 1908. Black church property also increased by more than 100 percent between 1890 and 1906, according to Du Bois's (1910) findings.

Homes are the single largest component of the average American's portfolio. Laurie Goodman and Christopher Mayer (2018) found that homeownership rates for black households have fallen every decade for the last thirty years. Goodman and Mayer (2018) also showed that black households with a college education were less likely to own a home than white households whose head did not graduate from high school. Their work also revealed that racial disparities in homeownership were not explained by income. The percentages of homeownership for white households was about 68 percent in 1985, 71 percent in 1995, about 76 percent in 2005, and nearly 71 percent in 2015. The percentages of homeownership for black households during the same time periods were 44 percent, 44 percent, 49 percent, and just over 42 percent. In short, there was an overall increase in homeownership between 1995 and 2005 and a decline between 2005 and 2015 and the percentages for black households were substantially lower than for white households in each year.

While there have been a lot of conversations of persistent racial wealth inequality in America there are still a lot of misconceptions about the extent to which there are black and white differences in the types and levels of assets owned. I was recently on a call where a financial advisor was sharing the details of an initiative aimed at growing black wealth. The black African man advisor dismissed any role that race might play in the relatively low levels of black wealth. The financial advisor said that no one cares about your race when you deposit money into an account. The financial advisor in question here conceded that he did not know much about the history of race in America but again felt at ease in dismissing it as an important, if not, central factor in understanding black asset poverty and racial wealth inequality in America. The data is clear, and research is abundant but far too many people, including many white people and the black financial advisor recently from Africa, do not fully understand or appreciate the legacy of racial discrimination and the roles of contemporary public policies in perpetuating and exacerbating racial wealth inequality in America, especially between black and white people.

## DOMINANT EXPLANATIONS

Scholars have been interested in studying wealth inequalities in America for years, including racial wealth inequalities between black and white people. W. E. B. Du Bois was among one of the earliest American scholars to study racial wealth inequality empirically. He attempted to dispel myths that black people had less wealth than white people because they were lazy. The fact that some black people had defied the odds and secured wealth was evidence that this was not the case. Instead, Du Bois pointed to the existence of an exploitative system, especially in the South that made black property ownership exceptional because black people had fewer economic opportunities and inherit less than white people.

Du Bois (1935) called for a better distribution of wealth and services in America. He thought that a more equitable distribution of wealth and services would leader to deeper art and wider intelligence. Du Bois (1935) warned of the looming of a new form of slavery. He contended that "the fact remains that Negroes are usually unwelcomed as physical neighbors, undesirable as fellow workers, unwanted in many schools, and additional liabilities in relief and insurance" (10). Part of the problem with the maldistribution of wealth was that white people in America simply did not "regard Negroes as equals; they do not wish them to receive the same income as whites; they do not want them advanced according to their ability and while they sincerely believe that the ability is not present save in sporadic cases they are often unwilling to test this fairly" (Du Bois 1935, 11–12). Du Bois (1935) called upon black people to support a program that would equalize wealth and eliminate economic classes.

Du Bois (1948) later warned about the worshipping of wealth in America. He argued that America moved from glorifying poverty to glorifying property. He called into question the ethics of property, wealth, and income. In many ways, Du Bois (1948) understood wealth as the sum total of the rationalized exploitation of workers. He cautioned the country against making greed their God (Du Bois 1948). Wealth, for Du Bois (1948), was critical to government control. In fact, he described this as a "persistent descent into hell" (Du Bois

1948, 3). Any society that places too much emphasis on wealth risked losing its culture and "the human soul" (Du Bois 1948, 3). Du Bois (1948) expressed a vital need to curb the power of wealth.

A year earlier, Du Bois (1947) commented on the myth of meritocracy as it relates to race and wealth. Du Bois (1947) stated, "The world has long assumed that this difference in power between the rich and the poor measures the difference in service to the public good; difference in accomplishment; in ability and in desert. And we have only to look around us to see that this is wretchedly untrue" (2).

Sometime later Du Bois (1953) commented on the future of black people in America. Du Bois (1953) defined the race problem as a struggle to vote, work, train for work, civil and social rights for black people. Du Bois (1953) made the case that America should measure prosperity not by the number of wealthy individuals but by the absence of poverty, the existence of good health, and equality of public schools, and widespread literacy. For Du Bois (1953) prosperity and by extension, progress, were not found in monetary gain but "progress is peace, and peace is time for food, homes for love, health for happiness and books to read" (12). Du Bois (1953) found it disheartening that too many Americans, many black people in America, were simply fighting for "a chance to live as human beings" (9).

Just prior to 1960, Du Bois weighed in about ongoing debates concerning solutions to poverty in America. Many Americans were concerned about socialism and communism and Du Bois (1958) said many Americans were misled into seeing either or both as evil and somehow criminal. Du Bois (1958) commented on the availability of physicians, hospitals, food security, and school for any child who wanted to attend. He warned against seeking revolution through violent means "but by truth and reason" (Du Bois 1958 9). In defense of workers Du Bois (1958) contended, "We must work but not exploit workers—by fare wages and recognize unions and wishes; we must encourage employment and cooperation in housing and buying; we should see that colored children are in school and assume responsibility for their work. We should encourage Negro art and history, not to antagonize but to inspire and teach. We should publish Negro books and encourage Negro art. We should regard Negroes as our own people" (9).

Oliver and Shapiro (1995) identified different structures of investment opportunities for black and white people in America. The authors advanced three important concepts: the racialization of state policy, economic detours for black businesses, and the sedimentation of racial inequality.

Oliver and Shapiro (1995) discussed some of the causes of racial wealth inequality in America to the extent that there exists two nations, one black and one white. Among the causes identified by Oliver and Shapiro (1995) were limited access to mortgage and housing markets. Additionally, Oliver and Shapiro (1995) said racial valuing of neighborhoods also contributed to past and present racial wealth inequality. The fact that banks routinely turn away qualified black people was another reason for racial wealth inequality. Additionally, Oliver and Shapiro's (1995) finding that black people were charged higher interest rates than their white counterparts and the existence of color coded housing values were also cited as predictors of racial wealth inequality in America. Given that homeownership is the single most important asset in accumulating assets the scholars estimated that institutional biases in the residential area costs black people over $82 billion.

Thomas Shapiro, Tatjana Meschede, and Sam Osoro (2013) identified several factors contributing to the racial wealth gap in America. The scholars observed that in 2009, for example, the median wealth for white families was about $115,000 compared to less than $6,000 for black families. The wealth gap tripled over a twenty-five-year period. Between 1984 and 2009 the gap increased from $85,000 to $236,000. The biggest drivers were years of homeownership, household income, unemployment, a college education, and inheritance. The scholars found that equal achievements did not result in equal rewards (Shapiro, Meschede, and Osoro 2013).

Scholar, Zainab Mehkeri (2014) highlighted the role of predatory lending in explaining racial wealth inequalities. Mehkeri (2014) showed how some mortgages were designed to default in the years leading up to the Great Recession and that these mortgages disproportionately affected black homeowners. The goal was to ensure profit for "collateralized debt obligations (CDOs)" (44). Consequently, subprime lending increased fivefold between 2001 and 2005, for example. More profits were earned when mortgages defaulted than when they were paid on time (Mehkeri 2014). Issuing subprime loans to people who qualified for prime loans was a process referred to as steering (Mehkeri 2014). More than 60 percent of subprime loans went to individuals who qualified for conventional loans. The unnecessary payments, according to Mehkeri (2014), led to massive foreclosures. There was a loss of black wealth ranging from $72 to $93 billion (Mehkeri 2014).

Neil Bhutta, Andrew Chang, Lisa Dettling, and Joanne Hsu analyzed data from the 2019 Survey of Consumer Finances and found that white families had eight times the wealth of the typical black family. The median wealth for white families was over $188,000, while the median wealth for black families was about $24,000. Bhutta et al. (2020) found that American families have yet to recover to their pre-Great Recession levels of wealth. They also found that the racial wealth gap widened over the life course. They showed that inheritance matters. Nearly 30 percent of white families received inheritances compared to only 10 percent of black families. Black families were also less likely to have retirement accounts and emergency savings. Bhutta et al. (2020) observed racial differences in equity as well.

# HISTORIC AND CONTEMPORARY PUBLIC POLICIES

## Slavery

Few periods had such a negative effect on black wealth generation as the period when physical slavery was legal in America. The first group of kidnapped Africans were settled in Jamestown, Virginia, in 1619. From the 1640s most black people were treated as chattel property. Even for those who lived their lives as free people of color, they faced obstacles in their quests to truly be free. Hundreds of laws were passed to restrict virtually every area of black life. On the one hand enslaved black people were a form of wealth generation for their slave owners and on the other hand free black people were limited in their abilities to build wealth for themselves and future generations. Slavery generated trillions of dollars for the United States economy (Copeland 2013). Slavery in Louisiana provides a good example of just how lucrative slavery was for slave owners and for the local and national economy and how devastating it was for the men, women, and children forced to live a life in bondage. I analyzed slavery in Louisiana in a self-published book about an ex-slave jockey named Abe Hawkins.

I observed that cotton may have been king in many places throughout antebellum America, but sugar was clearly the cash crop in Louisiana (Couvillion 2015). On average, Louisiana sugar plantations were valued at about $200,000, while the largest cotton plantations were worth about half that. In the mid-1800s, the highest concentration of millionaires in America could be found among plantation owners along the Mississippi River between Baton Rouge and New Orleans.

According to data on the history of slavery in Louisiana, most of the sugar grown in the United States, before the Civil War, came from the State of Louisiana. Louisiana produced a quarter to half of all sugar consumed in the United States. Sugar became the main crop largely because of technological improvements in the production of sugar. Slave revolts in the Caribbean were also a contributing factor to the growth of the sugar industry in Louisiana. The slave uprisings in the Caribbean led sugar producers and their slaves to places, like Louisiana (Hine et al. 2010). Etienne de Bore developed a technology for changing Creole cane into sugar. The technological advancement allowed for the conversion of cane juice into granules that could be shipped and stored more easily than conventional methods of the day. De Bore recruited slave owners who brought their slaves with them from places like Saint Dominque who had experience in converting cane juice to granules. Many of the slave owners were eager to come to Louisiana, as warfare between slaves and slave masters broke out on the island in the early 1790s, most notably the rebellion to free slaves. The rebellion was led by famed leader, Toussaint Louverture (Hine et al. 2010).

Technological advances in the production of sugar effected the number of people of African ancestry and their experiences on plantations. In 1830, more than 36,000 slaves worked in cane fields in Louisiana (Follett 2000). Within two decades, the number of slaves working in cane fields in Louisiana grew to more than 120,000. Nearly half of Louisiana's population was enslaved (Hine et al. 2010).

In *The Untold Story of Abe Hawkins*, I also observed that slaves were property and were bound to the land. They were valuable commodities owned by the enslavers owners. In 1770, bondsmen were valued, on average, at $400. Bondswomen were valued a little less at about $300. By 1790, enslaved men were valued at about $540 and enslaved women were valued at almost $500. In 1810, the average value of a male slave was more than $850. The average value of female slaves was about $670. Slave auctions were held as a way to liquidate estates and settle debts. Many auctioneers earned their livings facilitating the buying and selling of enslaved people ("Slavery in Louisiana," n.d.). One such slave auction took place in the Spring of 1840 where Jean Jacques Haydel sold more than sixty slaves for the price $57,000. Some of the slaves suffered from a variety of diseases and ailments. These ailments and illnesses including such things as hernias, swollen legs, and asthma. One of the slaves sold on that day was a young woman. She was sold for $2,650. She was described as thirty years old. She was a field hand with five children all under the age of eight, including a set of twins. The enslaved woman was sold to Felix Garcia.

The woman and other enslaved people sold at auction contributed to the booming sugar industry. Farm output, which was measured in hogsheads, increased over time as a result of the slave labor. In the early 1800s, for example, Louisiana produced about 5,000 hogheads. Hogheads were a large barrel used to hold about 1,000 pounds of sugar. By the mid-1850s, Louisiana produced almost half a million hogheads. Shortly thereafter, the total value of the sugar crop in Louisiana was worth $25 million ("Antebellum Louisiana II," n.d.).

In 1830, farm output averaged over 100 hogheads compared to about 270 in 1844 and 310 in 1853 (Follett 2000). In the early part of the nineteenth century, nearly two acres were cultivated per slave's hand. The number of acres grew from two acres cultivated per hand to 3.5 acres in 1822 and as many as five acres in the years that followed.

In the book, *The Untold Story of Abe Hawkins*, I wrote that work on the sugar plantations of Louisiana was rigorously policed. Slaves were central to the sugar industry often working from sun rise to sun set and in some instances, longer than that. The process of converting sugar required year-round labor. For example, on the Madewood Plantation, located in Napoleonville, Louisiana, work on the plantation was accomplished by "cycling slave workers through the cane shed at different points during the day and night, overseers assured constant sugar production and cruelly maintained the turning of the mills through the early morning hours" (Follett 2000, 12).

I showed that it was a common practice for slaves to work two eight hour-long shifts. John Hampden Randolph, a Louisiana planter, created a system of watches in the late 1850s. Randolph began his tenure as a planter in Mississippi growing cotton. A few years after marrying Emily Jane Liddell in 1837, he moved to Iberville Parish in Louisiana. He brought Dr. Henry A. Doyle's plantation, Forest Home, and continued planting cotton before switching to sugar in 1844. His partner was Charles A. Thornton. Randolph owned the land and Thornton provided the slaves, money, oxen, and mules. Randolph was to receive a portion of the crop as part of the arrangement. Randolph and Thornton remained partners until 1848, but Randolph continued acquiring property in Iowa, Wisconsin, and along the Mississippi River. The land he purchased near Forest Home was called Nottoway, where Randolph and his wife built a mansion, after the passing of Randolph's father-in-law. Randolph's wife received a sizable inheritance. Randolph soon entered into another partnership with a planter by the name of Franklin Hudson. This time Randolph acquired half of Blythewood Plantation, which Hudson owned (Shupe 2009).

Work on Randolph's Madewood Plantation was described as "brutally punishing for the bondsman, this labor regime hinged upon the imposition of a clock-ordered discipline where the working day was punctuated by formalized working rules-a regime that marched to the beat of the ticking clock" (Follett 2000, 12). Randolph's approach became the standard for extracting maximum labor from the bondsmen and bondswomen. An article published in 1850 in *Southern Cultivator*, advised planters to identify one or two cooks as a timesaving strategy. Slaves might spend upwards of an hour preparing meals. Samuel McCutchon of the Oakland Plantation in Plaquemine Parish, Louisiana, selected three elderly and sick women to prepare all the meals for the slaves on his plantation in 1859 (Follett 2000). Milly, a female slave with chronic joint pain, Beersheba, aged fity-eight, who suffered from an unidentified physical disability, and Betsy, who suffered from asthma, prepared meals for over 100 slaves on McCutchon's plantation. Planter William Minor was known to use bells and time signals in "regimenting the slaves' day" (Follett 2000, 13).

Before the shift from cultivating crops, like cotton and indigo to cultivating sugar, it was not unusual for slaves to clear land and plant crops like corn, rice, and vegetables. Slaves continued to do this type of work outside the planting and harvesting season. Slaves also built levees, served as sawyers, carpenters, masons, and smiths. Slaves raised horses, oxen, mules, cows, sheep, pigs, and poultry.

Sugar plantations in the South operated like factories in the North, but "the sugar masters neutralized their capitalist pretensions by retaining an ardent commitment to the lash and other archaic methods of antebellum labor discipline" (Follett 2000, 13). Corporal punishment was not uncommon. The formula for success, according to sugar planters, was force + discipline = economic success. Slave drivers recorded in their own words their commitment to using force to extract work out of enslaved men and women. Hunton Love, a slave driver on Bayou LaFourche plantation, recalled, "I had to whip 'em, I had to show 'em I was boss, or the plantation would be wrecked" (Follett 2000, 13). Andre Roman of a plantation in Ascension Parish, Louisiana, stated, "planters and overseers retained and frequently exercised the threat of physical coercion as a primitive, ancient, and unmerciful means to compel break-neck speed in the fields and mill house" (Follett 2000, 14).

Threats of physical violence were a daily part of plantation life in Louisiana. Many former slaves told of their experiences as part of the public work's program of the early 1900s. Former slaves, including Cecil George, told of threats and actual assaults. Reflecting on the horror enacted on enslaved men, women, and children, George characterized the United States as the most "wicked country God's son ever died for" (Follett 2000, 14). Jacob Stroyer, another former slave, described plantations as places "of slaughter" (Follett 2000, 14). A lot can also be gleaned from the accounts of visitors to sugar plantations during antebellum America. Most expected slaves to be "inferior" and "lazy" workers (Follett 2000, 15), but observed the opposite.

Slaves were indeed hardworking and desired freedom. Perhaps one of the greatest examples of the discontent associated with life on plantations in Louisiana is the slave rebellion of 1811, led by Charles Deslondes, which included some 500 slaves. Inspired by the successful uprisings in Haiti, and growing discontentment in the United States, slaves plotted for months to not only free themselves but also to dismantle the oppressive system of slavery. Deslondes led a group of slaves that grew in number as the rebellion expanded from what was referred to as the German Coast of Louisiana toward New Orleans. The freedom fighters targeted Manuel Andry's plantation. Marissa Fessenden (2016), writing for *Smithsonian Magazine*, wrote about one of the most important and arguably less talked about slave rebellions in United States history in an article published on January 8, 2016.

Fessenden (2016) observes the fighters demonstrated a commitment to the pursuit of freedom as evidenced in their resistance motto, "Freedom or Death." After wounding the planter and killing his son, Gilbert, the group of slaves went to the basement of the plantation mansion and gained access to weapons they might use in their efforts to free themselves and others. Armed with muskets, ammunition, and even militia uniforms, they pressed on towards New Orleans. Ideologically, the group felt a connectedness with the revolutionary actions of the enslaved in Haiti and other acts of resistance taking place on plantations along the Mississippi River between Baton Rouge and New Orleans. The militia attire symbolically linked the enslaved across geographical boundaries. Participants of slave rebellions in Haiti wore military-inspired clothes as they were engaged in a war against flesh, principalities, governments, injustice, and of course white supremacy ("A Clever Hero" 2011).

The march toward freedom lasted about two days along River Road. Research shows that the group burned abandoned plantations along the way. Research also shows that many of the freedom fighters were literate. Not only could some of those involved in the uprising read and write, but they also read very progressive and liberating literature (Fessenden 2016). Many were armed not only with muskets, ammunition, and machetes, but they were known to have copies of the French Declaration of the Rights of Man. Some of the fighters were battled tested having fought in civil wars in Ghana and Angola. One of the goals of the uprising was to establish a sovereign state.

The group was soon met by federal troops assembled to quell the resistance effort. Federal troops responded with brute force. Troops forced Deslondes and the others back near Jacques Fortier's plantation, in a town now named after Duncan Kenner's family. The militia made up of planters blocked the route of the bondsmen's retreat. The militia cut up the bodies of the bondsmen seeking freedom. Dozens of slaves were killed onsite. The slaves who managed to survive were eventually put to death by a firing squad. The skulls of the revolutionaries were placed on poles as warnings to other slaves who may be considering acts to dismantle slavery and/or seek freedom for themselves and family members.

The willingness of Deslondes and other slaves to risk their lives for the sake of freedom provides some of the best evidence of the horrors of slavery. Despite all of the evidence of the terror and violence that made slavery possible, far too many scholars, entrepreneurs, and private citizens have sought to (re)imagine and (re)present antebellum America and plantation in a positive light (Thomas 1992).

The horrors of the enslaved system did not end with the passage of three Reconstruction amendments. The adoption of the Thirteenth, Fourteenth, and Fifteen Amendments held out hope for former slaves. The Thirteen Amendment abolished slavery except in the case of the incarcerated and the Fourteenth Amendment was supposed to grant basic civil rights to former slaves, namely due process, citizenship, and equal protection. Formerly enslaved men were supposed to receive the right to vote with the adoption of the Fifteenth Amendment, but barriers were put in place to deny that right. Struggles to determine their destinies, including to build wealth remained.

## RECONSTRUCTION THROUGH THE EARLY 1900S

Thomas Shapiro, Jessica Santos, and Sylvia Stewart (2015) made the argument that "the Black-White racial gap is a structural, policy related created problem and it will require structural, policy-driven solutions" (3). The researchers also noted that wealth building for whites was almost always linked to the wealth stripping of indigenous people and the enslavement of Africans. They cited the Homestead Act of 1862 and Morrill Land Grant Act of 1862.

I described what I called the great land grab in "Race, Wealth, and Homesteading Revisited." I noted that white wealth was a direct result of many public policies. These policies included the removal of indigenous people. I described the 1830 Indian Removal Act, which expelled indigenous people east of the Mississippi River westward. I noted that prior to that time the 1790 Naturalization Act forbade nonwhites from becoming naturalized citizens. This meant that only citizens were allowed certain rights, such as the ownership of land ownership. Likewise, Alien Land acts kept nonwhites from owning or leasing land. Hence, some public policies created wealth for some, while prohibiting others from doing the same. The Homestead Act of 1862 was an excellent example. The act gave away millions of acres of land that was once part of territory owned and occupied by indigenous people west of the Mississippi. Estimates are that 270 million acres, or 10 percent of the total land area of the United States, was transferred to white people as part of the provisions for the Homestead Act provisions.

I noted that years the U.S. government simply gave away a quarter-section or a less quantity of unappropriated public lands to any white person who was the head of a family, or who had arrived at the age of twenty-one, and was a citizen of the United States, or who filed his declaration of intention to become a citizen, as outlined in the naturalization laws of the United States. The act also required that the individual had never taken up arms against the United States Government or supported any of the nation's adversaries. The homesteaders were to pay eighteen dollars and agree to live on the land for no less than five years.

The Homestead Act of 1862 has been described by scholars, including Dr. Tim Wise, as a classic example of whiteness shaping public policy and perceptions about public policy as it relates to race (Martin 2019). I concurred and argued that the Homestead Act of 1862 also shaped whiteness. It was an affirmation that whiteness meant citizenship and whiteness meant owning land (Martin 2019). According to Wise, while whites were the greatest beneficiaries of the act, the policy was viewed as an important mechanism for nation building and not as a form of entitlement for white people in the manner that historical and current programs, such as Temporary Aid to Needy Families and affirmative action policies, are often viewed as dependency programs for unworthy, unmotivated people of color, especially black people (Martin 2019).

Nonwhite people did eventually gain limited access to land through the enactment of laws such as the Southern Homestead Act of 1866. Under the 1866 act, individuals received title to the land after five years of residency and after showing that they had made some improvements (Martin 2019). Congress repealed the Southern Homestead Act in less than ten years. The 1866 version of the act was not regarded as successful given the relatively poor quality of land; white backlash to black landownership; dishonest practices; poor management by government administrators; and the homesteaders' lack of adequate resources (Martin 2019). Neil Canaday and his colleagues showed that more white homesteaders than black homesteaders were homesteaders in places like Louisiana (Martin 2019).

The floods in 1866 and 1867 in Louisiana did not help a system already fraught with challenges. The challenges facing the administration of the Southern Homestead Act of 1866 throughout the South, especially in Louisiana, included the understaffed and closed land offices and general poor oversight (Martin 2019). Claude Oubre argued that the white Democrats felt threatened by the very idea that former slaves might gain ownership of land that used to belong to former white planters, including those that supported the Confederacy (Martin 2019). Oubre also observed that, when homesteading was out of step with the interests of southern whites, even those who were moderately sympathetic to the plight of former slaves, whites aligned with railroad companies and turned away from any and all efforts to secure land for former slaves (Martin 2019). Oubre concluded that, while homesteading was not a success for whites or blacks, the failure to acquire land was much greater for black people and could best be described as a great tragedy (Martin 2019). Despite the fact that some former slaves had limited political and civil rights for a time, the absence of the economic empowerment that land ownership represented meant that their newfound rights and freedoms would not yield the return on investments for which they had hoped (Martin 2019).

Roy Copeland's (2013) work on African Americans and real property ownership revealed how some black people lost their land and the challenges they faced trying to acquire land. Copeland (2013) discussed how violence was used against black people who attempted to buy land as well as the outright refusal on the part of white people to sell to black people. Land ownership had great significance for black people. They understood land ownership as a "pathway to independence, and a confirmation of their freedom" (Copeland 2012, 646). Unfortunately, black people were duped by the state, legislatures, courts, white individuals, and white people as a whole when it came to land ownership (Copeland 2013).

One of the greatest betrayals occurred during the mid-1860s. On January 16, 1865, General Williams Tecumseh Sherman issued Special Field Order Number 15. He issued the order after meeting with a group of black clergy in Savannah, Georgia, to determine ways to support the large number of formerly enslaved black people following him and the people within his charge. Among the things the black clergy communicated that black people wanted was land and the right to determine their own destinies. To that end, Sherman issued a military directive which included the redistribution of 400,000 acres of Confederate agricultural lands. The lands were to be resettled by former slaves as a form of punishment to the Rebels. More specifically, the directive stated that the islands from Charleston south, which were largely abandoned rice-fields, that lied along the river to thirty miles black to the sea and the country bordering the St. John's River in Florida, were reserved for settlement of former slaves.

Sherman's order also stated that "At Beaufort, Hilton Head, Savanna, Fernandina, St. Augustine, and Jacksonville, the blacks may remain in their chosen or accustomed vocations." Sherman forbade white people from settling there with the exception of white military officers and soldiers on duty. He declared the black people there free and encouraged young black people to join the military's efforts. The order also described settlement by three parties who would then subdivide the land. The directive gave the former slaves possession but not ownership, some have argued (Copeland 2013). A government position was established to oversee the settlement system. Brigadier-General R. Saxton served as the Inspector of Settlements and Plantations.

Waymon Hinson explored black land ownership since Reconstruction and observed that black land ownership was at its highest in the early 1900s. After the early 1900s many Americans lost land, but black people lost land at a rate that was much faster than for white people (Hinson 2018). Hinson (2018) stated that black people lost land due to economic and technical changes that impacted all people and some that were unique to black landowners. Hinson (2018) identified seven themes that characterized the loss of land for black farmers, in particular. The themes included: heir property ownership, lack of estate planning, tax sales, partition sales, voluntary sales, no access to legal counsel, and other contributing factors. Hinson (2018) added other factors such as racism, restrictive government programs, discrimination by the United States Department of Agriculture, the Great Migration, and lack of local black leaders.

We also know that there were prosperous black communities in America during the early part of the twentieth century and some were violently destroyed. Chris Messer, Thomas Shriver, and Alison Adams, wrote about the destruction of the place many people called Black Wall Street. Messer, Shriver, and Adams (2018), described the thirty-five block community and the loss of about $8 million dollars (1921 dollars) in assets. The authors observed that it was black economic progress that was perceived as a threat by neighboring white residents. The community boasted some 10,000 residents and included nearly two hundred businesses. The businesses included drug stores, grocery stores, hotels, and a barbershop. The black community in Tulsa, Oklahoma, also known as Greenwood, had a library, two schools, a hospital, and a newspaper (Messer, Shriver, and Adams 2018). Allegations that a young black man, Dick Rowland, acted inappropriately with a white woman in broad daylight in a department store elevator, helped ignite what many call today a race riot. A white mob attacked the black community (Martin 2013). Police and National Guards officials sided with the white mob. Unable to defend itself, the black community was destroyed (Martin 2013). According to a commission on the race riots, twenty-six black people were killed, and ten white people were killed (Messer, Shriver, and Adams 2018) There are some estimates that as many as 200 people died in the rioting (Messer, Shriver, and Adams 2018).

## THE GREAT DEPRESSION, NEW DEAL, AND MASS ACCUMULATION OF WEALTH

Trevor Kollmann and Price Fisback (2011) were among the scholars to explore the New Deal, race, and homeownership in the first few decades of the twentieth century. Kollmann and Fisback (2011) examined how blacks and whites benefited from 1930s housing policies. The scholars found that white homeownership rates were higher in areas with more FHA mortgage insurance and fewer grants for public housing and slum clearance.

Shapiro et al. (2015) pointed to the effects of excluded agricultural and domestic workers from the New Deal. Black people were overrepresented in these occupations. They were therefore initially kept out of the New Deal. Black people were also kept out of one of the greatest periods of the mass accumulation of wealth in America.

Kenneth Jackson has conducted some of the most cited work on the role of real estate appraisals in the suburbanization of America, particularly the suburbanization of the nation by race. Jackson examined suburbanization in the United States between 1815 and 1980. The 1930s and 1940s were particularly important. Before the 1930s only the truly wealthy could afford to purchase homes. In many cases Americans had to pay for at least half of the value of the house and could arrange to finance the other half. Final payments were due within a relatively short time. After the establishment of the Home Owners Loan Corporation (HOLC) and the Federal Housing Administration (FHA) homeownership became more affordable for average Americans. According to Jackson (1980), "The HOLC replaced the unworkable direct loan provisions of the Hoover Administration's Federal Home Loan Bank Act and refinanced tens of thousands of mortgages in danger of default or foreclosure (421)." The HOLC granted loans at low interest rates to allow owners to get back their homes lost through forced sales, for example, showed Jackson (1980). Between July 1933 and June 1935, the HOLC paid out more than $3 billion for over a million mortgages or "loans for one-tenth of all owner-occupied nonfarm residences in the United States" (Jackson 1980, 421).

Jackson (1980) observed that before the HOLC homeowners were at risk due to the whims of the money market. The HOLC "systematized appraisal methods across the nation" (Jackson 1980, 422). Through the system of redlining, the HOLC facilitated the undervaluing of neighborhoods that were racially diverse or aging. Jackson (1980) outlined the four categories. The first category, A, was assigned the color green and considered the most desirable for new homeownership. The second category, B, was given the color blue. These neighborhoods were considered desirable. Jackson (1980) stated that the third category was C and yellow. The neighborhoods in this category were declining. The fourth category, or D, was the one assigned the color red. These neighborhoods were said to already be in decline. "Black neighborhoods were invariably rated as fourth grade" (Jackson 1980, 423). The HOLC supplied the grammar for real estate appraisals that involved the use of terms like infiltration and invasion (Jackson 1980).

Amy Hillier (2003) has a different perspective on the relationship between the HOLC and the practice of redlining. Hillier (2003) argued that lenders were avoiding the areas that were redlined before the HOLC and others began using the maps. Hillier (2003) stated that it was unlikely that the HOLC caused redlining. Hillier (2003) called the HOLC "as much a follower as a leader" in neighborhood appraisals (412). Hillier (2003) was not saying that the role of the HOLC was insignificant but misinterpreted. Hillier (2003) does not argue that the practices were race based and discriminatory toward black people regardless of whether the HOLC started the practice of redlining or not.

Jackson (1980) argued that the most damage was done by the influence of the appraisal system on other financial institutions, including the adoption of the system by the FHA.

The FHA was established on June 27, 1934, to address unemployment in the construction industry (Jackson 1980). Among other things, the FHA assisted with financing and established basic standards for home construction. Within a few decades the FHA assisted over ten million families in buying homes and another twenty million families improve their properties. The FHA also "hastened the decay of inner-city neighborhoods by stripping them of much of the middle-class constituency" (Jackson 1980, 433).

Shapiro et al. (2015) concurred with Jackson (1980) about the devastating roles of the HOLC, FHA, and the Veteran's Administration (VA), the latter excluding black veterans from higher education and the former organizations helping to fuel residential segregation.

## THE GREAT RECESSION AND CONTEMPORARY RACIAL WEALTH INEQUALITY

Another important period in the history of racial wealth inequality in America occurred during the 2000s and became known as the Great Recession. The Great Recession was marked by the potential failure of major corporations and industries and decline in wealth for average Americans regardless of race. The Great Recession had a far greater effect on the overall economic health of black people when compared with other groups are in large part due to the many risks they faced before the economic downturn in America. The Great Recession revealed, for example, that black people were at greater risk than other groups for predatory lending practices. Black people paid more for less (Martin 2013). Some media accounts "not only blamed the prevalence of such lending practices on the Great Recession, but some in the media also went as far as to blame blacks and other minorities, many of whom were victimized by lenders. . . . The overrepresentation of blacks, women, and low-income borrowers was observed prior to the Great Recession (Martin 2013 91).

An analysis of subprime lending of over 300 metropolitan areas revealed that subprime loans occurred among black people in more than 98 percent of them. Indeed, the NAACP initiated law suits against lending institutions arguing that the institutions "directly preyed upon blacks and other people of color. More precisely, the suit filed in Los Angeles against 14 lending institutions alleged 'systemic, institutionalized racism' in sub-prime home mortgage lending" (Martin 2013, 92). Additionally, the NAACP contended that black homeowners were substantially more likely to receive mortgages with higher-rate loans than similarly qualitied white home buyers (Martin 2013). This was the case even for black homeowners with relatively high incomes (Martin 2013). "A Wells Fargo employee admitted to what many had suspected that black applicants were preyed upon by the financial institution. . . . Some loan officers . . . referred to blacks as 'mud people' and referred to subprime lending as 'ghetto loans'" (Martin 2013, 93). The effects of the Great Recession on black people is still being felt.

Ongoing racial wealth inequalities have led some people to offer recommendations for narrowing the black-white gap. Among the proposed recommendations are reparations. Ta-Nehisi Coates wrote an oft-cited article on "The Case for Reparations." Andrew Kahrl (2019) also supports reparations but contends that current discussions must include the eleven million acres black people lost to fraud, deception, and theft, much of it in the past fifty years.

Shapiro et al. (2015) recommended the promotion of homeownership and broader investments into black communities. The scholars called for full-black employment and an end to mass incarceration. They also thought it was essential to promote school desegregation and make higher education more affordable to address the widening racial wealth gap in America. Moreover, Shapiro et al. (2015) called for increases to retirement securing for black people and fair credit practices that would put an end to predatory lending practices that disproportionately target black people. Shapiro et al. (2015) also expressed the need to adequately fund public institutions as a way of addressing the black-white wealth gap in America.

Laura Sullivan and Tatjana Meschede (2018) offered a number of recommendations for addressing the racial wealth gap in America. The scholars are among many others to call for support for black wealth building over the life course (Thomas et al. 2020). They advocated policies tailored to people of color. Sullivan and Meschede (2018) also called for expanded homeownership and fair lending practices. Financial buffers for lower wealth householders was also suggested.

Courtney Boen, Lisa Keister, and Brian Arsonson (2020) asked scholars and others to look beyond net worth as the country attempts to address the racial wealth gap. Boen and their colleagues (2020) link race, wealth, and health. They found that racial differences in portfolios mattered. Savings, stock ownership, and homeownership improved health (Boen et al. 2020). Conversely, debt was associated with worse health. The scholars also found different health returns to assets by race. Hence, Boen et al. (2020) contended that there was a complex relationship among race, wealth, and health. To address the finding that the median net worth for white households was twenty times that of black households, Boen et al. (2020) suggested that greater attention should be devoted to building liquid assets and promoting homeownership because together these factors would yield the greatest health returns. They also called for systematic change aimed at building and/or redistributing wealth. Boen et al. (2020) showed that intervention was necessary to close the racial wealth gap in America, which should lead to greater economic and racial health equity.

Keith Dye advocated for reparations and showed how the call for reparations was not new. For decades black people have debated about ways to make reparations a reality. Dye (2020) chronicled debates among black people about whether black capitalism or socialism was the appropriate framework for expanding black wealth. Dye (2020) described the 1969 Black Manifesto. The document was part of the Black National Economic Conference. In it the group described how they were compelled to assemble because "racist white America has exploited our resources, our minds, our bodies, our labor. For centuries we have been forced to live as colonized people inside of the United States, victimized by the most vicious, racist system in the world. We have helped to build the most industrial country in the world" (Black Manifesto 1969, 1). The group demanded $500,000,000 from white Christian churches and Jewish synagogues for their roles in the subjugation of black people. They argued that the estimate was very low. They estimated that this amounted to about $15 for every black person and represented only the beginning of addressing the debt owed to black America. The Black National Economic Conference outlined how the money should be spent. They called for the establishment of a Southern land bank to assist black people who want to relocate and establish cooperative farms. They asserted the need for land ownership. The group demanded $200,000,000 to fund the land bank.

The Black National Economic Conference also wanted four major publishing and printing industries with a price tag of $10,000,000. The locations for the proposed publishing outlets were New York, Los Angeles, Detroit, and Atlanta. The group anticipated that the industries would "help to generate capital for further cooperative investments in the black community, provide jobs, and an alternative to the white-dominated and controlled printing field" (Black Manifesto 1969, 2).

Another way that reparations could be spent is through the creation of four audio-visual networks to combat negative representations of black people in the white dominated press. Moreover, the group demanded $30,000,000 for a research skills center to aid in the understanding of the extent of the needs of black people in America (Black Manifesto 1969). Additionally, money should be spent on a training center. At least $10,000,000 was requested for a site that would teach a host of skills, ranging from community organizing to communication.

The group expressed an interest in collaborating with the National Welfare Rights Organization. They also demanded $10,000,000 for welfare recipients and shared plans to organize welfare workers to appeal for more money and greater efficiency in the administration of the welfare system.

The Black National Economic Conference also asked for $20,000,000 to create a National Black Labor Strike and Defense fund. The fund would support black workers who were fighting against racists conditions in their work environments. The Conference demanded the establishment of the International Black Appeal (IBA) and identified this as one of the most significant demands. With at least $20,000,000 the IBA would work to generate more financial resources to fund cooperative businesses both in the United States and in countries in Africa. IBA would be led by James Forman and be responsible for raising money for the Conference, developing cooperatives and supporting the African Liberation Movement, and establish the Black Anti-Defamation league to control the images of people of African ancestry. The Conference also demanded the establishment of a black university located in the South with the sum of no less than $130,000,000.

The Conference leaders acknowledged the need for broad support for their stated demands. To that end, the Conference stated that all black people should consider themselves members. They called upon black people familiar with the manifesto to share the demands with other black people in their networks highlighting the need for the reparations as outlined. The Conference did not underestimate resistance to their demands and invited members to engage in protests to bring attention to the demands, which they described as both modest and reasonable.

Jeff Kaufin and Janet Novack (2021) identified five ideas to narrow the racial wealth gap. Kaufin and Novack (2021) anticipated that the current pandemic would widen the gap. They called for directing capital to black businesses. Kaufin and Novack (2021) observed that black businesses tend to lack access to capital and often fund their businesses with their personal credit cards. The scholars also supported the issuance of baby bonds to everyone and called for federal student loan forgiveness in the amount of $10,000. Kaufin and Novack (2021) explicitly supported reparations to the descendants of slaves and funding to help Americans establish and/or build emergency savings. While some of the ideas set forth by Kaufin and Novack (2021) were intended for all Americans, some were specific to black people. The scholars recognized the relative disadvantaged position of black people when compared with other groups, namely white people in America. Kaufin and Novack (2021) stated that more than 70 percent of white Americans but only about 40 percent of African Americans could get $3,000 from family or friends in the event of an emergency. These groups tend to be racially homogeneous, which further highlights the need for economic justice and not mere charity.

Susan Kuo and Benjamin Means (2021) were among others to call for reparations for black people in America. They presented a rationale for reparations and used corporate law to make their case. Kau and Means (2021) conceded that for reparations to be a reality that the nation would have to combat the principle of ethical individualism. The principle "holds that people can be blamed only for their own actions" (Kau and Means 2021, 800). They acknowledged that opposition to reparations was largely based on passage of time and individual responsibility. Many Americans, including many white Americans, contend that too much time has passed since slavery ended and that most people alive today were not directly responsible for what happened many centuries ago. These arguments ignore the continuing significance of race, including the many ways that white people today benefit from the racialized social system that was created before the nation was even founded. Kau and Means (2021) concluded that individual ignorance was of no significance because the responsible person was the entity itself, in this case, the United States, a legal person.

Renuka Rayasam and Ben White (2021) contend that President Biden must address racial wealth inequality if he was truly serious about remembering the roles that the black electorate played in his successful presidential bid. Rayasam and White (2021) observed that wealth levels for black people with a college education, for example, declined by nearly half when compared with white people between 1989 and 2016. Rayasam and White (2021) recommended federal contracting with black businesses as one strategy for addressing the racial wealth gap in America.

Any effort to address persistent racial wealth inequality in America will involve dispelling widely held myths about the causes and consequences. Dion Rabouin (2021) identified ten such myths. According to Rabouin (2021) the myths included the idea that closing the racial wealth gap was possible through education, personal responsibility, homeownership, individual accomplishments, increased savings, black banks, black businesses, financial literacy, emulating model minorities, and strengthening families. Black homeowners, for example, tend to carry more mortgage debt and receive less returns on their investments into homeownership. Educated black people, black people who are employed or married consistently have lower levels of wealth or no wealth at all.

Catarina Saravia identified the need to address low United States rates. Saravia (2021) argued that low US rates actually make the racial wealth gap worse. Savarvia (2021) found, for example, that gains in stock prices that come with lower interest rates disproportionately benefit white Americans.

Valerie White, executive director of LISC NYC, a community development financial institution weighed in on how best to address the racial wealth gap in a 2021 op-ed piece. While White (2021) commented on the state of black and brown people in New York City, White's (2021) suggestions may be applicable to black communities across the nation. According to White (2021), there must first be a recognition of the root cause of the racial wealth gap. White (2021) cited policy choices and the treatment of black people as second-class citizens. Thus, White (2021) contended that a systemic approach to addressing the racial wealth gap was required. For White (2021) it involved acknowledging the role of race in decision-making processes on a daily basis. There must be a focus on racial justice and equity from hiring to purchasing, for example.

White (2021) argued that deliberate action was required to close the racial wealth gap. Initiatives must target black communities specifically. There must be a movement from broad based economic development to what White (2021) called economic transformation. White (2021) cited investments into broadband access in black neighborhoods, commercial rent relief for black business, and capacity-building for nonprofit and community-based organizations that support black businesses.

Finally, White (2021) advocated for sustainable wealth generation. White (2021) said sustainable wealth generation must be prioritized. Sustainable wealth generation would be possible with support for the expansion of black homeownership and black business ownership. Both would build generational wealth, according to White (2021).

## RACIAL REALISM AND RACIAL WEALTH INEQUALITY

Many people struggle to understand how and why racial wealth inequality exists and persists. Racial realism provides a great deal of insight in explaining why the racial wealth gap between black and white people has increased over time despite historic and contemporary court cases, initiatives, and policies that might predict otherwise. Derrick Bell asserted that racial equality should not be the end goal in the ongoing struggle for racial justice. He observed the problems with America's courts and other institutions that were rooted in the existence of a racialized social system that subordinated black people. Bell contended that despite apparent peaks of progress that little would change because of the racialized nature of America's institutions and because of the unwillingness on the part of some Americans to see black people as their equals. Consequently, black people would forever remain in a subordinate position and only experience small victories when such actions benefited the dominant racial group in America and only under those circumstances. When one embraces Bell's claims and arguments it becomes clear why racial equity as it relates to wealth has eluded black and white Americans for all of the nation's history.

*Chapter Three*

# The Myth of the Greatest Generation

Black men and women have participated in every American war. They have fought for their liberation and the liberation of others all the while facing racial oppression. The liberation struggle took place both on American streets and court rooms but also on battle fields both in the United States and abroad. Many black Americans believed that their military service would lead to better treatment, including full citizenship and recognition of their humanity. Historically, this has not been the case. This chapter examines the roles of black men and women in the military beginning with the American Revolution through present-day service. Special attention is devoted to an analysis of the men and women who served in World War II and lived during this era who are often referred to the Greatest Generation. I explore what is meant by this phrase. Next, I debunk the myths associated with this idea, namely I question how this generation could be called the greatest given that antiblackness all but ruled the era. I discuss how black people were duped again as it relates to military service and why racial realism is an important tool for unpacking these important issues.

The National Center for Veterans Analysis and Statistics chronicles the history of black men and women and their military service. It is noted that both enslaved and free black people, for example, fought in the American Revolution, which began in 1775 and ended in 1783. About one-fifth of the colonial population at the start of the Revolutionary War were black men. James Armistead was one of those men. Born enslaved in Virginia, Armistead volunteered for the army. He delivered messages between the French units and later became a spy. Armistead's work contributed to America's victory in the Battle of Yorktown. Armistead was not only awarded full military honors when he died but was also granted his freedom. This would not be the case for all black people who served during the American Revolution or for black people more generally. In all, about 5,000 black people served in the Colonial Army ("Minorities in the Military," 2017).

The National Center for Veterans Analysis and Statistics also documents the heroic sacrifices of black soldiers during the Civil War, which took place between 1861 and 1865. More than 200,000 black people fought in the Civil War, most of them in the Union Army, but also in the Union Navy. The War Department approved the 54th and 55th Massachusetts Colored Infantry Regiments at the request of Massachusetts Governor John Andrew. The Center describes two members of the 54th Massachusetts, William Carney and Martin Delaney. Carney was born enslaved in Virginia and later served as a color bearer. It is noted that during the fight at Fort Wagner in South Carolina that Carney kept the flag from touching the ground. Carney was wounded more than once and has the distinction of being the first black person to receive the Medal of Honor.

Martin Delany, who later worked with the Freedman's Bureau, an agency established to assist former slaves, among other duties, was the highest ranking black officer in the Union Army. He founded, "The Mystery," a black newspaper, and gained admission into Harvard Medical School. Protests by white students forced Delany out before he could complete his first year. Once the 54th Massachusetts was established, Delany recruited black people to join the fight. In 1865, President Lincoln promoted Martin Delany to major of the 104th US Colored Troops where he served.

Black women also played important roles in America's many wars. Lucy Higgs is one example. According to the National Center for Veterans Analysis and Statistics, Higgs joined the 23rd Indiana Regiment near Bolivar, Tennessee. Lucy Higgs was the only black and only woman in the regiment. She traveled throughout the South serving as a nurse. Despite her service, Lucy Higgs encountered barriers when she applied for a nurse's pension. She was denied. A Special Act of Congress was needed for Lucy Higgs to finally receive her pension.

Robert Smalls is also highlighted in the history of black soldiers in the report published by the National Center for Veterans Analysis and Statistics. Like Delany and Carney, Smalls lived life in physical bondage. Enslaved in Beaufort, South Carolina, Smalls was the Navy's first black captain. The report describes how Smalls took advantage of an opportunity to take over a rigger, named, the Planter, that was used for cargo and special deliveries. About eight enslaved people were part of the crew. When the Planter's captain went to Charleston, Smalls took control of the vessel surrendering it a close by Union blockade. Smalls joined the US Navy. Smalls later became an elected official both on the state and federal levels, representing the people of South Carolina.

The National Center for Veterans Analysis and Statistics estimates that more than 37,000 black soldiers died or more than one-third of all black soldiers who served in the Civil War. Despite their hopes that the abolition of slavery and enactments of key amendments would lead to full citizenship and recognition of the humanity of black people, racism endured.

According to Henry Louis Gates, black people were very committed to serving in the military and many undoubtedly shared W. E. B. Du Bois's (1918) hope that by doing so black people as a whole would secure greater rights. Du Bois, editor of *The Crisis,* wrote about black veterans returning from World War I. There were black veterans on the staff at black publications and organizations, such as *The Messenger* and Marcus Garvey's United Negro Improvement Association. Du Bois regularly received and published letters from black veterans. Du Bois (1919) observed, "As the war destructively demonstrated, race, nation, empire, and militarism formed an inextricable nexus" (361). He commented that "No man has ever seen the Negro fighting at his best, because the Negro has never yet fought for himself" (Du Bois 1919, 361).

Gates, however, pointed to the hypocrisy that defined the nation. While black people were willing to serve they received little support from their government. For example, President Woodrow Wilson showed the pro-KKK film, *Birth of a Nation,* in the White House and refused to sign an anti-lynching bill. All the while, over two million black people registered for the draft during World War I. The Marines did not accept them. The Navy enlisted some but only in menial positions. Most served in the Army. More than 400,000 black soldiers participated in World War I, between 1914 and 1918 or 13 percent of active duty soldiers with about 200,000 deployed overseas as part of the American Expeditionary Force and the French Army. Eugene Bullard was one of the black soldiers who fought in World War I. He was the first black and the first American combat fighter pilot, according to the National Center for Veterans Analysis and Statistics. Bullard served in the French Air Force and was excluded from serving in the US Army Air Service because he was black.

Joining Eugene Bullard in serving during World War I were black soldiers, Henry Johnson and Needham Roberts (Sammons and Morrow 2014). Johnson and Roberts served in the 369th Regiment made up mainly of black men soldiers from Harlem, a group of valiant fighters who were often left out of history books and nostalgic war movies (Garcia 2014). The regiment spent over six months on the front lines and spent more time on the front lines than any other American unit. Johnson and Roberts fought off a German unit while themselves wounded and later received France's highest award for valor, the Croix de Guerre award. Johnson, for example, was posthumously awarded the Purple Heart and Distinguished Service Cross and was recommended, more recently, for the Medal of Honor, according to the National Center for Veterans Analysis and Statistics (2017) and Richard Sheposh (2020). "Johnson himself became a champion for his fellow troops testifying before the New York State legislature in early 1919 in support of a bill to give veterans a preference in government hiring" (Trickey 2018).

Only a few black people were permitted to serve as sailors during World War I, such as John Henry Turpin. It is noted by the National Center for Veterans Analysis and Statistics that black people would not be permitted to serve as sailors again until the early 1930s and in very limited roles, serving almost exclusively in mess halls and as stewards.

The participation of black veterans in World War I did not lead to their enjoyment of full citizenship or bring about the recognition of their humanity and the humanity of all black people despite black challenges to the racial status quo. Gates recorded that on August 23, 1917, black soldiers in the 24th Infantry Garrison in Houston revolted after an assault by police. Indeed, racial discrimination persisted within the military and in the broader society. In fact, the years following World War I were some of the most violent against black people. In 1918, there were sixty-four documented lynchings. In 1919, there were eighty-three. In 1919, there were riots across America, including in Chicago, Washington, D.C., Knoxville, Congview, Texas, Phillips, Arkansas, and in Omaha, Nebraska. The year 2021 marked the 100th anniversary of the massacre in Tulsa, Oklahoma, where the prosperous black community was burned to the ground, sparked by a white woman's claim that Dick Rowland, a black man, sexually violated her in an elevator in the middle of the day.

This is also evidenced in the experiences of black soldiers during World War II. They experienced racial discrimination during the course of the service both within the military and outside of the military. World War II took place between 1941 and 1945. The National Center for Veterans Analysis and Statistics cites Doris Miller as on the first heroes of Pearl Harbor. Although Miller's responsibility was to carry wounded soldiers to safely, he operated an anti-aircraft machine gun during a battle. The report also chronicles the story of the historic Tuskegee Airmen. The group was one of the most respected escort groups for Air Form bomber pilots. They were credited with taking out more than 200 German aircrafts and nearly a thousand supply vehicles. Erick Trickey (2018) wrote that the regiment "fought a war for a country that refused them basic rights and their bravery stood as a rebuke to racism, a moral claim for first-class citizenship" (2).

Beth Bailey and David Farber (2001) wrote about the dual campaign fought by black veterans, especially those serving in Hawaii during World War II. Bailey and Farber (2001) recalled the call published in the *Pittsburgh Courier* where the editorial board called "upon the President and Congress to declare war on Japan and against racial prejudice in our country. Certainly, we should be strong enough to win both of them" (817).

Bailey and Farber (2001) stated that between December 7, 1941, up until late 1944 Hawaii was under martial law. More than a million personnel and civilian employees were on the islands of Hawaii. About 30,000 Americans of African descent were among them working as soldiers, sailors, and war workers. Prior to their arrival there were very few black people there. According to Bailey and Farber (2001), there were only two hundred black people in Hawaii in 1940. Myths about black people were spread across the state mostly by white Southern soldiers. The myth that black people lacked the intelligence and discipline to serve was spread. There were concerns that the mere "presence of blacks might create or exacerbate local racial tensions" (Bailey and Farber 2001, 822). Evidence showed that white soldiers warned that "blacks were, literally dangerous animals" (Bailey and Farber 2001, 825). Local women would not sit next to black men on buses. They were told that black people were not to be trusted. They were also told that black people had tails and that they gave birth to monkeys. Black people were framed as not really American. Despite some efforts on the part of people like Lt. Delos Emmons to dispel such myths and create a more equitable for black people serving in Hawaii, his orders did not seem to affect the experiences of black people serving in the Pearl Harbor shipyard and other Pearl Harbor work and housing areas, for example. Housing was segregated as were such places as barbershops. Although mess halls, theaters, and commissaries were integrated, white Southerners were "furious over the government's call for fair and equal treatment" (Bailey and Farber 2001, 832). Between 1942 and 19455, there were four riots.

The presence of the 369th Regiment and their many successes helped challenge the myths about black soldiers and about the larger black population (Wigger 2021). The fighters have been the subject of many scholarly articles and books. Bailey and Farber (2001) described them as highly skilled combat soldiers. Part of their training included combating racism in towns like Oswego, New York. Their experiences exposed the need for the Double-V campaign. For example, in 1941, a white woman said she was raped by a black man. The entire unit was lined up and searched. This led to a boycott of Oswego. Charges against a black man were eventually dropped. Black soldiers in the 369th Regiment, and black soldiers more generally, had to navigate their dual status as black and as combat soldiers.

The Double-V campaign did not end when the war ended although, many black veterans expected change after returning from war (Clark 2020). The life and legacy of Johnnie Jones of Baton Rouge, Louisiana, is a good example. Jones participated in World War II and was even wounded. In 2021, he was awarded the Purple Heart. After completing his service as a soldier, he later graduated from Southern University Law School and became an integral part of civil rights fights in Baton Rouge, Louisiana. He played an important role in the historic 1953 Baton Rouge bus boycott.

In the early 1950s, Louisiana forbade black people from owning bus lines, which meant that black residents had to ride the public system. Shortly after banning black people from operating bus lines, fares were increased in Baton Rouge. The ridership was made up largely of black people traveling from their neighborhoods to predominately white areas where they worked largely as domestic servants. The buses were segregated by race. Black people in Baton Rouge were forced to the back of the bus and forced to stand even when the front section, which was reserved for white people, was empty. The Reverend T. J. Jemison, pastor of Mt. Zion Baptist Church, was among the community leaders to address the problem. He and others appealed to the City Council and were successful in getting the body to pass Ordinance 222. The ordinance allowed for seating to take place on a first come, first serve basis irrespective of race. The mostly white men bus drivers refused to enforce the ordinance even after becoming aware of it. The white men bus drivers threatened a strike and received support from the Secretary of State who deemed the ordinance to be in conflict with other state and federal laws. Upset at the turn of events, the black people of Baton Rouge refused to ride the buses. They developed a car riding share program. The program involved donations of gas and the use of personal vehicles to transport black residents to work and other places they needed to go. The bus boycott had a negative effect on the revenue generated by the public bus system. A compromise was reached allowing for first come, first serve seating. The back seat was reserved for black riders and the front seat was designated for white riders. While everyone was not pleased with the outcome of the nearly one-week long boycott, the actions of the black community in Baton Rouge provided a blueprint for the 1955 Montgomery bus boycott that lasted far longer, introduced the Reverend Dr. Martin Luther King, Jr., to the world, and ended segregation on buses in that city and across the South. Johnnie Jones, a World War II veteran, was the legal counsel on this and many other civil rights matters during the 1950s and the 1960s in Baton Rouge.

Rockwell (2001) wrote about the significant roles of black veterans following their participation in the World Wars in a 2001 article published in the *New York Times*. Rockwell (2001) described what he called the racial militancy of black veterans after the conflicts. There was a "warlike nature of American race relations" embodied in black veterans, such as Chad Williams. He and others represented the New Negro—a group of black people that refused to accept the racial status quo without challenging it. Black veterans questioned the meaning of their service and developed new ways for achieving racial justice. Black veterans, according to Rockwell (2001), were key figures in the history of the New Negro movement and the civil rights movement. Iconic civil rights leader, Medgar Evers, who was assassinated at his home for his efforts to call attention to various forms of antiblackness in America, was a war veteran, noted Rockwell (2001).

Researcher Ruth Lawlor (2019) wrote about the overrepresentation of black soldiers. Lawlor (2019) addressed the complex history of World War II. Lawlor (2019) stated that the war should not be reduced to a victory of democracy over fascism. Lawlor (2019) observed that Germany fought for white supremacy, while the U.S. maintained a segregated army that treated black and white veterans differently especially when it came to allegations of criminal activity. Lawlor (2019) said this was a part of the history that remained untold. During World War II, forty-six soldiers were charged with rape and twelve of those charged were black (Lawlor 2019), although black soldiers only made up 10 percent of soldiers. Lawlor (2019) highlighted the legacy of racism. Black soldiers were often scapegoated. Black soldiers were two-thirds of those found guilty of crimes. Lawlor (2019) wrote, "Rape was the fertile ground on which issues of racial segregation were weaponized and used as an instrument of wartime politics. The history of the good war is incomplete without acknowledging this aspect of our past" (7).

As of 2020, the seventy-fifth anniversary of the end of World War II, about 300,000 American World War II veterans were living. A total of sixteen million people served. About 350,000 women served and 14,500 of them were still alive today (Schaeffer 2020).

Black soldiers fought during the Korean Conflict. Taking place between 1950 and 1953, the Korean Conflict, as it is described by the National Center for Veterans Analysis and Statistics, involved North and South Korea. The United Nation's force supported the South and China fought for the North with assistance from the former Soviet Union. The Center notes that the Korean Conflict was the first conflict fought with troop integration. The disbanding of the 24th Infantry Regiment signaled the end to segregation as an official policy in the Army. William Thompson who was posthumously awarded the Medal of Honor for his service during the Korean Conflict becoming the first black person to receive the honor since the Spanish-American War in 1898.

Black people served again during the Vietnam era. Between 1960 and 1973, North Vietnam fought South Vietnam. North Vietnam was aided by the former Soviet Union and China, among other countries. The United States aided South Vietnam. The United States was concerned about the emergence of new communists countries and greater influence on the part of the former Soviet Union should the North and South reunite. The National Center for Veterans Analysis and Statistics mentions the heroics of Clarence Sasser. He was a medical aidman. Sasser aided many wounded soldiers despite being wounded himself and was later awarded the Medical of Honor.

Black men and women continued to participate in the military after the Vietnam era through the present day including after September 11, 2001 and during peacetime. Data for 2018 published by the U.S. Census Bureau revealed that nearly 12 percent of veterans of the all-volunteer force era identified as black. About 15 percent of post-9/11 veterans were black compared to 16 percent of Gulf War veterans and 17 percent peacetime only veterans. An article published in the *New York Times* in May 2020 written about Helene Cooper commented on the hypervisibility of black people in the military and the invisibility of black people at the highest levels. Cooper observed that about 43 percent of the more than one million men and women on active duty in the U.S. military are people of color. The decision makers at the time of her writing were almost all white and male. In the spring of 2020, just two of the forty-one highest commanders in the military were black, General Michael Garrett and General Charles Brown, Jr. Cooper cited the widely and long-held belief that black people as a group were not fit to lead. For the relatively small numbers of black officers many are relegated to transportation and logistics and steered away from combat specialties that serve as a pipeline to the most senior commander positions in the military. Cooper also mentioned a survey of more than 1,600 active duty subscribers to the *Military Times* which found that more than half of minority service members witnessed white nationalism or racist ideology among white troops.

Of all the veterans who have served, World War II veterans receive some of the most positive press and the valorization of World War II veterans has extended to the entire generation. The myths and romanticizing about the so-called Greatest Generation mask the role that this generation played in perpetuating racism in America both in the military and beyond.

In the introduction to a memoir of World War II veteran, Walter Hobson Crockette, Loren Pennington (2012–2013) provided some insight as to why the cohort became known as the Greatest Generation. Pennington (2012–2013) wrote that the birth cohort grew up during the Great Depression. "They became great in the press of war, and the values and attitudes they took on in wartime continued with them for the rest of their lives" (Pennington 2012–2013, 235).

This generation remained silent as black veterans and black people more broadly were kept out of the single most important period of the mass accumulation of wealth in America. White Americans in this generation fought the integration of buses and schools, among other areas of public accommodation. Perhaps the manner in which the GI Bill denied the vast majority of black veterans access to benefits readily available to white veterans provides the best example as to why the nation must reconsider how the cohort is memorialized.

Scholar David Onkst (2001) wrote about the GI Bill and observed the various actors that "helped perpetuate one of America's greatest myths—that the GI Bill of Rights positively transformed the lives of an entire generation of America's war veterans" (517). Onkst (2001) described this as an oversimplification and described the limited effect of the bill on black veterans. He observed the optimism shared by black veterans and their high expectations. Onkst (2001) recounted the mistreatment black service people experienced in the Army and Navy, including at the hands of white officers.

Onkst (2001) focused on black access to the GI Bill between 1944 and 1948. Onkst (2001) pointed to the roles of racial discrimination and poor administration as factors contributing to black veterans unequal access to the GI Bill. The bill was supposed to be available to veterans who served at least ninety days without a dishonorable discharge. Onkst (2001) outlined the four benefit areas. The bill was intended to assist veterans with finding jobs, receiving unemployment benefits, accessing loans, and obtaining a college education or vocational training. While many described a New South characterized by new defense industries the racial policies and practices of the region remained relatively unchanged. To be clear, black people experienced racism across the country. Onkst (2001) elected to focus specifically on the South.

The absence of black counselors at local Veteran's Administration Centers served as a barrier to black veterans accessing services. In 1947, there were only a dozen black counselors in George and in Alabama and no black counselors in Mississippi. Given that decision-making authority was granted at the local level this was a tremendous problem for black veterans who were forced to engage with white counselors who did not see them as equals despite their military service. Here was yet another example of a seemingly race-neutral bill that effected people differently because of their race. For example, white counselors routinely denied black veterans with general or blue discharges which were common for black people labeled as troublemakers for engaging in protests aimed at ending segregation (Onkst 2001, 520).

Onkst (2001) also noted that white counselors refused to refer black veterans to skilled and semi-skilled jobs. "Whites got 86 percent of the professional, skilled, and semi-skilled positions. Blacks, conversely, were forced into 92 percent of the unskilled and service-oriented jobs" (Onkst 2001, 521). Onkst (2001) added that to white counselors "any job, no matter how menial or poorly paid, was 'suitable' for black veterans" (521).

Black people in general encountered problems dealing with local banks and this was true for black veterans as well. While the GI bill allowed the federal government to guarantee loans it did not actually lend money to veterans. Applicants had to secure loans from a bank, and they needed collateral. Given the relatively disadvantaged position of black people and black veterans prior to their service it is not surprising that they did not have the required collateral and there were no guarantees that their race would not matter and work against black veterans. Mississippi was a good example. Black people made up half the population but only one of the thirty-six loans to veterans between June and December of 1946 went to a black veteran. In 1947, of the more than 3,200 loans guaranteed to veterans in the state, only two went to black veterans.

Onkst's (2001) research showed that veterans needed on-the-job instructors in order to get vocational training. White employers, Onkst (2001) observed, often refused to work with Southern black veterans. Onkst (2001) noted that white employers feared competition from trained black veterans. Onkst (2001) also noted that the lack of adequate funding for site inspectors meant a lack of accountability for discriminatory employers, for example.

Black veterans benefited from the establishment of black run leagues, such as the Georgia Veteran's League. Veterans often advocated for more respect and services from their government, but black veterans were not welcomed in many all-white veterans groups, including Christian veterans groups. Black leagues faced many challenges including calls from groups like the NAACP to desegregate white veterans organizations instead of creating black veterans groups. Black leagues also feared being labeled as communists and all of the negative consequences associated with the label. Black veterans also had some success in obtaining training at Historically Black Colleges and Universities (HBCUs), however, many were already struggling financially due to inadequate funding, which contributed to such things as overcrowding and limited housing options.

Onkst (2001) concluded, "the tragic part of the story remains that Southern black veterans, despite their expectations and the federal government's promise, were unable to secure their rightful entitlements, even though the veterans throughout the country were able to use the GI Bill to significantly improve their lives" (Onkst 2001, 534).

Scholars Sarah Turner and John Bound (2003) also analyzed the GI Bill and the effects on World War II veterans by race. They explored whether there were similar effects on college attainment for black and white men as many have assumed and as many black men had hoped. Turner and Bound (2003) also explored whether region mattered. They observed that President Theodore Roosevelt met with black leaders in September 1940. Roosevelt supported black people in the military and the segregation of black and white troops, according to Turner and Bound (2003). In 1940, there were six black units representing about 4,500 soldiers. Additional facilities were built to keep black and white soldiers forcibly separated. The Serviceman's Readjustment Act of 1944, known more commonly as the GI Bill, appeared "race-neutral," as others have suggested (Frey 2016; Turner and Bound 2003), but the evidence suggested that race mattered. Turner and Bound (2003) found that for every year of birth analyzed that white veterans had higher levels of educational attainment than black veterans born in that same year. For example, white veterans born in 1920 had on average 11.4 years of education at the end of their service compared to 7.5 years of education for black veterans born in 1920 at the end of their service. White veterans born in 1924, for example, had 11.4 years of education compared to 9.6 years for black veterans. White veterans born in 1929 had about eleven years of service, while black veterans born the same year had ten years of education.

Turner and Bound (2003) showed that not only did race matter but region mattered as well, especially for black veterans. Black veterans in the South lagged further behind white veterans than in other regions.

Robert Jefferson conducted research on the relationship between race, disability, and World War II. Disabled veterans as a group often faced challenges in making sure their needs were met but this was especially challenging for black veterans with disabilities (Jefferson 2003). Jefferson's research showed how "VA physicians and administrators implemented a means tests that combined racial perceptions of African Americans with cultural views associated with people with disabilities" (1104). Moreover, Jefferson contended that "the history of the development of service-related disability policies in the twentieth century often reflected nonclinical evaluative practices couched in cultural and racial values" (1104). Black veterans, according to Jefferson, were viewed negatively and many VA physicians and administrators thought they should be grateful for any level of service they received even if it was below what they were entitled to receive. VA physicians and administrators claimed black soldiers were inherently more likely to suffer from upper respiratory diseases, sexual transmitted diseases, and emotional disorders (Jefferson 2003). The disability claims of black veterans were often dismissed or minimized by attributing their suffering to prewar experiences (Jefferson 2003). In the end, black veterans received "official help but unofficial hostility" (Jefferson 2003, 1111). To add insult to injury, black veterans with disabilities were excluded from the largest veterans with disabilities groups and found the most success when they created their own organizations, like the United Negro Allied Veterans of American organization, which drew attention not only to the plight of black veterans with disabilities but also to employment, lynching, voting, and housing issues facing the broader black population (Jefferson 2003).

It should be noted that some scholars have argued that the GI Bill was successful even for black veterans. Ira Katznelson and Suzanne Mettler (2008) were at odds in their assessments of the GI Bill for black and white veterans and addressed how two scholars could reach different conclusions. Katznelson's work has led him to the conclusion that the GI Bill was as one black veteran stated, for white veterans only. Katznelson (2008) stated, "For sure, African Americans were not excluded by the formal terms of the legislation. But its terms of administration and its pathways for participation widened the racial gap and reinforced an American tragedy" (531). Mettler (2008) analyzing different data holds that the benefits were inclusive across racial lines. She described the bill as having "comprehensive and universalistic qualities" (Mettler 2008, 520).

Sophie Frey's (2016) work on black and white veterans and the GI Bill supported Katznelson's (2008) overall assessment. Frey (2016) agreed that the vast majority of beneficiaries were white veterans and that any benefits to the overall economic well-being of black veterans should be attributed to the legislative victories of the civil rights movement and not to the GI Bill. Frey (2016) made the claim after analyzing data from 1940–1990.

Denise Bostdorff (2003) examined how former President George Bush leveraged myths about the World War II generation in his characterizations of the attacks on September 11, 2001, and the ways in which he hoped the nation would respond. Bostdorff (2003) observed that Bush asked the younger generation to keep the national covenant of the World War II generation. Bush depicted evil as the cause of the attacks on 9/11 not as an effect. He "depicted a benevolent God and placed primary blame for the nation's problems on external sources rather than on his 'parishioners'" (Bostdorff 2003, 294). Bostdorff (2003) described Bush's style as a "rhetoric of covenant renewal" (298). Bush described the United States as blameless and exceptional and claimed the nation was attacked because of its goodness" (Bostdorff 2003, 299). This same characterization may be seen in noted network news journalist, Tom Brokaw's books (1998, 1999), *The Greatest Generation* and *The Greatest Generation Speaks: Letters and Reflections* and filmmaker Steven Spielberg's *Saving Private Ryan*. Bostdoroff (2003) also cited scholar Robert Putnam's *Bowling Alone,* where Putnam expressed concern about declines in social solidarity and in service to others. Putnam claimed that the World War II generation did more than their share of service (Bostdoroff 2003). Films like *Saving Private Ryan appeal to emotion and moral virtue as contemporary American depictions of wartime sacrifice and trauma (*Burnetts 2016). Burnetts (2016) showed how such films reflect cinema's nostalgic mystic pasts or golden ages.

Bostdoroff (2003) showed how President George W. Bush often made comparisons between the threats faced by the World War II generation and the 9/11 generation. The two were juxtaposed as the greatest generation and the lost generation. Bush intentionally referred to the nation as America instead of as the United States to further endear people to his claims that the country was targeted because it is the "brightest beacon for freedom and opportunity in the world" (Bostdorff 2003, 302). Bush went as far as to equate Al Qaeda and other non-domestic terrorists with the World War II enemies of the past. Bostdorff (2003) argued that Bush's decision to compare the attacks on 9/11 with the events surrounding and including World War II was intentional. According to Bostdoroff (2003), Bush chose a so-called good war over more controversial wars, such as the Korean and Vietnam Wars. Bush did not mince words. He stated that the evil from World War II had returned and that America's cause was renewed. Bush spoke very little about ongoing racial disparities at home or about U.S. foreign policy that may have contributed, even in some small way, to the attacks on American soil.

The lynchings of black men in uniform are historical facts that are often untold. My colleagues, Stephen C. Finley and Biko Gray (2019), and I wrote about lynchings in an article published in *Issues in Race and Society* and how they may best be understood even in contemporary times.

We argued that violence was, and still is, used as an important tool to maintain the system of physical bondage, to infringe upon the civil rights of people of African ancestry, to enforce segregation, to stabilize a system of intellectual hegemony, and to maintain a racialized caste system for the generations that followed (Hine, Hine, and Harrold, 1999; Michael 2009; Morris 1984). Antiblack violence was aimed at reinforcing and legitimating myths about white supremacy and black inferiority, which included efforts to criminalize and control black populations (Fanon 1952). Among the most horrific and sadistic examples of the use of violence as a form of torture and terrorism rooted in antiblack sentiments were the many acts of mob violence occurring between Reconstruction and the 1960s (Gray, Finley, and Martin 2019, 150).

We also noted that just as definitions of mobs have changed over time, so too have definitions of lynchings changed over time (Tolnay and Beck 2018). For a time, scholars looking back on white mobs focused primarily on the gratuitous violence against black bodies that united and stabilized white communities and reinforced the racial status quo in America with a particular focus on key actors (Tolnay and Beck 2018). Lately, scholars have reconsidered whom to include as participants in white mobs (Ohl and Potter 2013). White people—men, women, and children included—both angrily and cheerfully participated in lynchings and racism across the country both actively and passively, that is, through inaction and tacit support (McLaughlin 2007; Prince 2017; Yancy 2004). Increasingly, conceptualizations of white mobs expanded to include individuals, groups, and institutions complicit in the domestic terrorism aimed at black people in America across the South and the North (Ohl and Potter 2013). Thus, white mobs must include witnesses refusing to identify perpetrators, journalists publishing defaming stories about black people or refusing to publish stories about white mob violence (Ifill 2003; Yancy 2004; Gray, Finley, and Martin 2019, 151–152).

We further contended, "WVMs seek to maintain and justify White supremacy and assault and terrorize Black bodies, communities, and institutions. WVMs, like those of their forefathers and fore-mothers, rely upon the complicity of a broad spectrum of White people and predominately White institutions to continue to harm Black people in material, physical, psychological, political, and professional ways" (Gray, Finley, and Martin 2019, 152).

Many black people sincerely believed that serving in the military would lead to better treatment and more rights. They were duped into believing that their willingness to serve their country would win them favor with their government and ordinary white citizens. "On the other side of African American hopes were fears that black veterans asserting, and demanding equality would disrupt the social order built on white supremacy and the racialized economic order from which many benefited" ("Lynching in America" 2017, 8). Perhaps the greatest manifestation of the white fear described here was the lynching and other forms of terrorism experienced by black people in America, in this case black veterans of the Civil War and the World Wars ("Lynching in America" 2017).

The Equal Justice Institute published a report about lynching in America with a particular emphasis on the targeting of black veterans. In fact, the report identifies black veterans of the Civil War, World War I, and World War II as the most at-risk group within the black population for violence and racial terror. Their mere presence in uniform signal for many white Americans the possibility of the dismantling and disruption of Jim Crow laws and overall racial subordination ("Lynching in America" 2017).

The Equal Justice Institute estimates that thousands of black veterans were assaulted, abused, and threatened after their military service. The institute focused primarily on lynchings and other assaults that took place between 1877 and 1950. The report described a black veteran by the name of Hosea Williams. Williams became a well-known civil rights advocate. He recalled being captured by the Germany Army and remarked that they treated him more humanely than the state troopers of Alabama ("Lynching in America" 2017).

Not only was the sight of black men in military uniforms viewed as a threat to old ways of doing things, but the presence of black veterans also conjured up old fears that armed black people would enact their revenge against the white people who had oppressed them and their ancestors for hundreds of years. The Equal Justice Institute documented efforts to keep black people from owning guns. Some states made it a crime for black people, including black veterans, to own guns and knives, for instance. In Florida, there was a rule in 1866 that prohibited black people from possessing a gun. The offense was punishable by a public whipping ("Lynching in America" 2017).

The white media often played a central role in misrepresenting images about black people and encouraging the hysteria associated with white fears of perceived black progress. In May 1866, a group of white people attacked a black community and the newspaper blamed it on black gun ownership ("Lynching in America" 2017). During the massacre, black people were raped, maimed, and killed. Additionally, black churches, homes, and schools were burned to the ground ("Lynching in America" 2017).

The Equal Justice Institute provided many examples of the lynchings of black veterans and the overall reign of terror aimed at black communities. Peter Branford, a black veteran, along with other black veterans, was killed in Mercer County, Kentucky. A mob took his clothes, beat him, cut off his penis, and forced him to run half a mile to a bridge outside of town where he was then shot and killed ("Lynching in America" 2017).

On August 19, 1898, James Neely was wearing his uniform when he went to a drug store to get something to eat. Neely protested when told to order at the back of the store and not the front. A mob chased him and shot at him. Neely was later found dead of gunshot wounds ("Lynching in America" 2017).

"Lynching in America" (2017) highlighted the public spectacle that characterized many lynchings of black people, including black veterans. On January 15, 1901, Fred Alexander, a black veteran of the Spanish-American War was accused of assaulting a white woman and blamed for the death of another white woman, Pearl Forbes, killed two months prior to claims made against him. Alexander was burned alive as a crowd of thousands gathered to watch the vigilante killing.

The report also documented the finding that more than a dozen black veterans were lynched after World War I. In Pine Bluff, Arkansas, a white woman ordered a black veteran off of a public sidewalk. When the black veteran responded that he would not move, and that the U.S. was a free country a mob soon formed. The black veteran was tied to a tree with tire chains and fatally shot fifty times ("Lynching in America" 2017).

On February 13, 1946, Hugh Johnson, a twenty-one-year old black Navy veteran was accused of assaulting a white woman and was beaten by the Ku Klux Klan ("Living in America" 2017). A few months later on August 8, 1946, John C. Jones was lynched in Minden, Louisiana. It was alleged that he looked into the window of a white family. He and his cousin were beaten to death. On August 17, 1946, JC Farmer was waiting for a bus in Wilson, North Carolina. He was questioned by police. He wanted to know why the police were questioning him as he had done nothing but be in uniform and waiting for a bus. JC Farmer was brutally beaten by police and shot. Farmer died an hour after his engagement with the police ("Living in America" 2017).

# RACIAL REALISM AND BLACK MILITARY SERVICE

Racial realism provides the best explanation for understanding why so many black people over the course of American history have believed that behavior modification would somehow make white people treat them better. In this case, some of the greatest black intellectual thinkers on the subject of race, such as W. E. B. Du Bois, encouraged black people to join the military and built up their hopes that doing so would lead to more rights and to racial equality. The enactment of certain legislations, such as the GI Bill, built up the expectations of black veterans for a better life than the one they left before their service. As the bulk of the research on race and the GI Bill has shown, racial disparities existed and persisted in the implementation of the policy. The fact that being black and wearing a uniform put one at great risk for experiences of overt antiblackness revealed that no matter what black people did or did not do mattered little. What mattered was their race. Black identity, as Derrick Bell has shown, was and is associated with subordination. If you understand racial realism then you understand why black people believed that change would come, fought to be the change they wanted to see, and were disappointed when their status at the bottom of the well remained unchanged.

In the next chapter, "(Un) Civil Rights and Black Power," I contend that much has been written about the legislative successes of the civil rights movement and the effects of the Black Power movement. Despite the promises of both movements, black people continue to lag behind white people on a host of social and demographic outcomes. Again, black people were duped. Racial realism illuminates how the primary strategies of this era were actually ineffective and point to the perpetual subordination of black people in America. I provide insights that support Bell's claims.

*Chapter Four*

# (Un)Civil Rights and Black Power

In this chapter, "(Un)Civil Rights and Black Power," I contend that much has been written about the civil rights and Black Power movements, including by and about icons such as Dr. Martin Luther King, Jr., and Kwame Ture, formerly known as Stokely Carmichael.[1] Despite the contributions of both movements and sacrifices of both men, black people continue to lag behind white people on a host of social and demographic outcomes.

Both King and Ture believed that the experiences of black people in America could change by nonviolent strategies or by black people getting together and taking care of business. King and Ture and black people as a whole were duped. I argue here how King has been used and misused to justify the historical, unequal treatment black people received and continue to receive in the U.S., especially within the context of American civil religion. This has also been the case for the man who led the largest black movement in the United States prior to the civil rights movement, Marcus Garvey. King and others believed, at least for a time, that the United States government and its white citizens could change, and black people would eventually experience equality. Garvey's movement foreshadowed and likely heavily influenced the Black Power movement.

Next, I show how Kwame Ture and Charles Hamilton (1992), authors of *Black Power*, share King's optimism about upsetting the racialized social system and thus freeing black people from their subordinate position. Ture and Hamilton (1992) outlined a framework for achieving black power in their classic book, which was first published in 1967.

Finally, I show how one particular group, and leader, represents a departure from the hope that King and Ture had in the likelihood that the United States would change the racial social order. It can be shown that the Nation of Islam (NOI), founded more than ninety years ago, especially under the guidance of Ministers Louis Farrakhan, foreshadowed and perhaps later embraced what Bell (1992) described as racial realism. This is best shown in Farrakhan's description of an encounter with an unidentified flying object

(UFO) and scholarly interpretations of the meaning of the account (Finely 2012, 2013). This is also evidenced in a July 4, 2020, speech, "The Criterion," that Farrakhan delivered where he talked about a range of topics including racial injustices and the pandemic. I conclude by arguing that racial realism best illuminates how King and Ture raised the hopes of many black people in America and their unwillingness to fully acknowledge the perpetual subordination of black people in America did little to change the plight of the majority of black people. The NOI's refusal to believe that a nation built upon hypocritical creeds would ever change is far more in line with racial realism than the civil rights or Black Power movements and is perhaps why the NOI remains both intriguing and misunderstood.

The civil rights movement in America occurred throughout much of the twentieth century. Among the often cited victories of the civil rights movement were the *Brown v. Board of Education* U.S. Supreme Court decision in 1954, the 1955 Montgomery Bus Boycott, 1964 Civil Rights Act, 1965 Voting Rights Act, and the 1968 Fair Housing Act. These so-called victories did not fundamentally change the racialized social structure in America, especially the subordinate status of black people. Black people continue to see the need to proclaim black lives matter because mounting evidence points to the fact that in far too many cases they do not. Not only was the civil rights movement limited because of all the hope it held in the nation's ability and willing to change but it was also misused to justify the ongoing mistreatment of black people. This is perhaps best illustrated in debates about King and American civil religion and whether a black civil religion in America even exists.

For example, Jana Weiss (2019) offered commentary on King and what he called the pitfalls of American civil religion. Weiss (2019) described conceptualizations of black people as a chosen people within a chosen people. "King evolved as an interpreter of a highly critical, African American civil religion influenced by the African American jeremiad" (Weiss 2019, 435). Weiss (2019) added that American civil religion has done more harm than good to King's legacy. Linkages between American civil religion and King's legacy "has distorted and muted King's radical message of social change, rendering his call for political activism obsolete" (Weiss 2019, 447).

Another example of the misidentification of critiques of American society as reflective of some form of American civil religion is found in Randall Burkett's work on Marcus Garvey. Burkett (1978) described Garveyism as a religious movement that institutionalized a black civil religion. Garveyism "provided a common set of shared beliefs and value commitments which sought to bind its adherents—all those men and women of African descent who proudly too the name Negro—into a collectivity which was divinely called to a task in the world" (Burkett 1978, 67). Garvey was able to accomplish this, at least in part, by making sure people from separate denominations would participate in Universal Negro Improvement Association (UNIA) activities. Garvey used symbols, rituals, and beliefs that were rooted in their shared experiences and build upon the shared experience of slavery and history of racial discrimination and interpreted it into

> the light of a transcendent goal: the uplift of the Negro race and the redemption of Africa. They stood as symbols of national solidarity, binding all men who willing accepted the . . . term Negro into a single people whom God had specifically chosen for the task of building up a nation in Africa—a nation capable, first, of securing that continent's freedom and, second, of ensuring the rights of Negroes wherever they might reside in the world. (Burkett 1978, 67)

Tracey Hucks (2014) has written about religious nationalism, which more aptly described what people like King, Garvey, and others were doing. Specifically, Hucks (2014) outlined "forms of religious nationalism that mobilized around hermeneutical conceptions of Africa that affected religion, history, culture, style, language, and ideology" "(Hucks 2014, 8). Hucks (2014) revealed the various "ways African Americans sought to re-own or repossess Africa through textual reflection and religious expressions that centered Africa as the progenitor of a reestablished history" (8). They rejected the "socialized ontological deficiency" that was thrust upon them, while firmly believing in their own identity (Hucks 2014, 24). Embracing the beauty of blackness, even the idea that God was black, "is not only theologically defensible, but is a necessary corrective against the power of domination" (Hucks 2014, 24). Garvey, like King, was politically focused but also used religious and theological approaches in "rehumanizing pejorative impressions of blackness" (Hucks 2014, 24). Religious nationalism, argued Hucks (2014), "redresses . . . historical problems of black more essence, ontological heathenism, and spiritual pathology" (40). Religious nationalism, not American civil religion, or even a black American civil religion, facilitated both racial and religious agency with an emphasis on "the inner side of the color line" (Hucks 2014, 41). Religious nationalism provides African Americans with a space of transcendence by moving beyond politics, economics, and nationhood. "Its quest is often for a place of shelter from the political disenfranchisement, bodily invasion and assault, and socioeconomic and identity trauma visited upon people of African descent" (Hucks 2014, 45).

While Burkett (1978) was correct in his assessment that Garvey is misunderstood and the reasons why, namely that he was often understood through the eyes of his critics, he mislabels Garveyism as a form of American civil religion when it is more accurately placed within the framework of religious nationalism.

Despite the criticisms, there seems to be no documented criticism of the idea that American civil religion actually endured three trials. This implies that American civil religion at various points in American history was at risk. I argue that what Bellah called trials, including the three I added, are better understood as *peaks of panic*. I draw upon the work of Derrick Bell (1992) in making this claim. Bell (1992) wrote on many subjects, including racial realism. Bell (1992) reflected on the history of race in America. He wrote about historic periods where it seemed as though black people were making great strides toward becoming more included in American society. These periods included the end of physical bondage and various legislative victories. The legislative victories, such as the landmark *Brown* case, the Civil Rights Act of 1964, and the Voting Rights Act of 1965 were supposed to end the forced separation of black and white people in schools, in areas of public accommodation, and remove barriers to the ballot. Nevertheless, schools remained separate and unequal. Black people continued to face racial discrimination in many areas of public life, and access to the polls remained a challenge. Bell (1992) understood these historical moments as peaks of progress and not as fundamental changes that altered the racialized social structure that has characterized America for much of its history. Bell (1992) argued that understanding that the more things seemed to change, the more things really stayed the same and in some instances got worse. Embracing this reality, for Bell (1992), would lead to an avoidance of feeling a sense of disappointment in the lack of actual progress on racial matters in America. Bell (1992) assured those committed to social justice that there was satisfaction in the fight but reminded them that the outcome of then and future battles was already known. The powerful would only concede power so long as it was in their interest and in ways that would not alter the racial status quo.

We can think about Bellah's (1965) trials in a similar way. The perceived threats to whiteness, to American civil religion, were indeed just perceptions. The trials associated with the American Revolution, the Civil War, the modern civil rights movement, 9/11, the Great Recession, and the election of President Obama and protests about COVID-19 stay-at-home order were merely periods of panic on the part of white people in America. They were moments of intense fear followed by overt acts of public rage, but they were by no means evidence of any threats to American civil religion.

Contemporary colorblind ideology is an important feature of American civil religion. Colorblind ideology serves to protect whiteness and promote a myth of inclusion while promoting exclusion. The contemporary origins of colorblind ideology are often traced back to Dr. Martin Luther King, Jr.'s historic *I Have a Dream* speech, delivered at the March on Washington. The focus on a few lines from the speech is indicative of a methodological problem that befell Bellah's (1965) work on American civil religion. Bellah (1965) chose to focus on a few selected documents to substantiate the existence of an American civil religion. While American civil religion exists, support for its existence is not only found in the words of a few documents and speeches written and uttered by presidents but more importantly it is supported by the actions of many individuals, some with legitimate governmental authority and others who have been deputized by virtue of being considered white. A few lines from King's speech have been used and misused in a similar way to support American civil religion and colorblind ideology. This is particularly clear when one examines the debates about the establishment of holiday in King's honor.

Helm's claimed the holiday would be too expensive costing the nation upward of $5 billion. Helm also argued that King was a proven Marxist, and thus un-American and unworthy of a national holiday.

Arguably, the people of Arizona put up the most opposition to the King holiday (Alozie 1995). Arizona was the last state to approve the King holiday and the only state to bring the matter to a popular vote. In 1986 Governor Babbit authorized a paid King holiday for state employees. Governor Mechanan later rescinded the holiday. The state endured a boycott by the National Football League (NFL) for their refusal to honor the holiday. Commissioner Taliagues moved the Super Bowl from Tempe, Arizona, in protest.

An examination of King's written and life's work beyond the speech show that while he hoped for a time in America's history where race would not be the determining factor in the life chances and life opportunities for anyone, especially for black people, that he favored race-specific solutions to race-specific problems. This is evidenced in King's support for black power.

Many historians and non-historians like to frame King and calls for black power as oppositional when in fact King had much to say about the value of promoting black power. While it is true that King did not favor the use of the term, he did not denounce the sentiment. King was far more concerned with how the white press and white Americans would misinterpret the meaning. King (1967) makes this clear in his book, *Where Do We Go from Here?*

In his book, King (1967) described how the phrase black power was introduced into the movement. King (1967) stated that the phrase was first used within the movement in Greenwood, Mississippi, during the James Meredith Freedom March. The march began with James Meredith and was continued by others following Meredith's near-death experience. Meredith was shot fighting for social justice issues. In *Where Do We Go from Here?*, King (1967) assessed the values and what he saw as the liabilities of the term. King (1967) acknowledged that black power was a response to the use of white power. White power was degrading of black people and thus the term black power "had a ready appeal" (King 1967, 30). King (1967) understood that the utterance and meaning of the phrase black power aimed to "build racial pride and refute the notion that black is evil and ugly" (King 1967, 31). King (1967) highlighted some of the ways in which white power signaled that greater value was placed on the lives of white people than on the lives of black people, such as in the deaths of people connected to the movement. This was true in the ways that white public officials and the white press reacted to such deaths. King (1967) also expressed disappointment with white Christians who he said appeared "to be more white than Christian" (36).

King (1967) was not the one-dimensional symbol for race-neutral policies and programs as his legacy is framed today. On the contrary, King (1967) understood that the root of the so-called Negro problem was not of his own making but was the result of an "indelible imprint of inferiority," that was the result of a history that "has been soiled by the filth of worthlessness" (39). King (1967) believed that one goal of black power was "to resurrect joyously the African past" (41). Like Bell (1992), and others, King (1967) was skeptical about just how meaningful legal decisions and legislations could be in changing the racial contours of American society. This is clear when he articulated, "No Lincolnian Emancipation Proclamation or Kennedyan or Johnsonian civil rights bill can totally bring this kind of freedom" (King 1967, 44). In essence, King (1967) was signaling the limit to which American civil religion could reach. In other words, it was not designed to extend to black people, and this is particularly important because a number of scholars have not only associated King (1967) with colorblind ideology but also with American civil religion.

To be clear, King (1967) was also critical of black power. He did not agree that separatism, an idea some adherents to black power ideology embraced, was the answer to America's race problems. He thought separatism contained within it "seeds of its own doom" (King 1967, 45). He felt that alliances with the majority group were important but over the course of his brief life, he became increasingly skeptical about their effectiveness and sincerity.

Mary Frances Berry's work also showed that King did not endorse colorblind ideology. On the contrary, Berry (1996) stated that "civil rights advocates insisted that while color-blindness was a goal, remedies for discrimination could use race to get beyond the effects of racism against African Americans" (139). King and others were denounced when they advocated for change beyond neutrality, argued Berry (1996). They faced accusations that focusing on group discrimination violated American individualism.

King (1967) found value in black power and he spoke positively about a host of race-specific initiatives. King (1967) spoke and wrote about the merits of affirmative action, reparations, and structural economic change. "For victims of racial oppression, specific social, economic, or legislative remedies are required," King argued (Berry 1996, 143).

Not only is King misremembered as a champion for race-neutral approaches to black-white challenges but his association with American civil religion is also misplaced. American civil religion is a mechanism for justifying white privileges and overall black disadvantage. American civil religion unifies members of the dominant racial group across a variety of social differences. King and his life's work should not be considered as part of American civil religion or a black form of American civil religion.

King's views on race are part of a separate and larger tradition that is uniquely black. Frederick Harris is among the scholars to describe this tradition. Harris (1999) examined the empowering effect of religious culture on black political mobilization. He focused on how culture matters and understands culture not as a mediating factor but an independent contribution. In an effort to broaden the resource mobilization perspective regarding social movements, Harris (1999) argued, "that the indigenous culture of politicized groups facilitates the construction of meaning for action" (134). African American religion, which was created for and by African Americans, "provides sacredly ordained legitimacy to political action" (Harris 1999, 135). African American Christianity speaks "directly to the structures of oppression with causes of black suffering" (Harris 1999, 136), which American civil religion does not and cannot do because its aim is to promote and consolidate whiteness at the expense of blackness and black people.

African American religion, not American civil religion with which some scholars have tried to associate with King and his thoughts on race, helps black "actors make sense of political goals by developing indigenously constructed meanings drawn from shared worldviews, languages, religion, experience, and history" (Harris 1999, 136). Whereas, in American civil religion God is present in African American religion "God himself is politicized" (Harris 1999, 153).

King's association with colorblind ideology and reduction of his life's work to a few lines in a historic speech are just two of many issues in understanding efforts to explain ongoing racial disparities without adequately addressing race. Michael Brown and his colleagues (2003) described colorblind ideology as a way of whitewashing race. The scholars said beliefs about race rest on the following tenets: (1) The civil rights revolution was successful. (2) Racial differences persist because black people do not take advantage of opportunities. (3) The United States is becoming colorblind. Brown et al. (2003) also observed that benefits for white people were so natural that they are taken for granted. Racism is misunderstood and viewed as a remnant of the past. "A very different picture emerges when racism is understood as a sense of group position and as the organized accumulation of racial advantage, a system best understood by observing actual behavior" (Brown et al. 2003, 43). Moreover, Brown et al. (2003) contended that "much of the opposition is based on resentment toward blacks, and the resentment is driven by a fear (conscious or not) that the interests of whites as a group are jeopardized by color-conscious policies" (56).

The law supports the benefits of being white in America. "The law and large institutions normalize white advantage by articulating and enforcing cultural norms, which help to maintain racial hierarchy in the United States" (Brown et al. 2003, 56). Colorblind ideology, argued Brown et al. 2003, "has become a powerful sword and a near impenetrable shield, almost a civil religion, that actually promotes the unequal status quo" (58).

The consequences of embracing colorblind ideology as opposed to color-conscious programs and policies are far-reaching. Michael Buozis addressed some of the consequences in a 2018 article about police violence in Baltimore. Buozis (2018) said colorblindness is "crippling the ability of those in urban governments to reform police conduct and procedures, to institute civilian review boards, and to make sure police charged with brutality and homicide will see impartial judges that are not influenced by those state governments resisting the sweeping changes needed" (48).

There are a number of examples of colorblind initiatives. The introduction of Proposition 54 in California in October 2003 is just one example (Chow and Knowles 2015). Proposition 54, known as the Racial Privacy Initiative, would have prohibited state and local governments from classifying individuals by race, ethnicity, color, or national origin for the purposes of public education, public contracting, and public employment. The proposed law could be applied broadly to all state operations. The legislature could make the case that the collection of race-specific data was necessary by two-thirds of both houses. The signature of the governor would also be required. Law enforcement, court orders, and consent decrees would be exempt. According to the proposition, supporters of the Racial Privacy Initiative claimed checking a race box was demeaning, divided people, and increased attention on physical characteristics, such as skin color and national origin. Opponents of the Racial Privacy Initiative kept racial disparities private. The proposition did not pass but received millions of votes in support of it.

## WHY WHITE BACKLASH

White backlash is a dangerous thing. King (1967) wrote extensively about white backlash, far more than he wrote or spoke about his oft-quoted dream. King (1967) identified white backlash as the true source of black disadvantage in America. King wrote, "It would be neither true nor honest to say that the Negro status is what it is because he is innately inferior or because he is basically lazy and listless or because he has not sought to lift himself by his own bootstraps" (King 1967, 71). King added, "to find the origins of the Negro problem we must turn to the white man's problem" (King 1967, 71). King (1967) placed the responsibility of the status of black people at the feet of white people.

King (1967) understood white backlash as an expected outcome of the racialized American social structure as opposed to some occasional anomaly enacted upon black people by a few extremists. King (1967) highlighted the role of religion in the oppression of black people in America, an observation that points to the group's wholesale exclusion from American religion, which used religion to create walls of protection around whiteness and American civil religion. King (1967) wrote, "Religion and the Bible were cited and distorted to support the status quo," and he wasn't referring simply to the days of slavery but throughout time. King (1963) was publicly critical of white clergy for their roles in maintaining the racial status quo during his lifetime. King's famous, "Letter from the Birmingham Jail," was just one of many places where he offered a scathing critique of white Christians, especially white church leaders.

King authored the letter in April 1963 in response to letter (shown as an advertisement) placed in a national newspaper by a group of Alabama clergy representing every major world denomination. In the letter the clergy described a nonviolent campaign in Birmingham as both unwise and untimely. The clergy thought more negotiations were more prudent than direct action. Peaceful demonstrations would only incite hatred and violence, the group argued. They encouraged law enforcement to keep the city safe from violence and urged black people in the city to withdraw their support. Racial change in the city should come through the courts and not by way of the streets.

King (1963) issued a response, authored primarily from solitary confinement in a Birmingham jail cell. King (1963) addressed claims that direct action was inappropriate and poorly timed (Carson 1998). He also addressed accusations that King did not belong in Birmingham because he was not from the city, a claim King dismissed on the basis of his organizational ties and his commitment to fight justice anywhere in the U.S. (Carson 1998). King (1963) likened himself to the Apostle Paul who went about sharing the gospel of Jesus Christ. King said he was "compelled to carry the gospel of freedom beyond" his place of birth (Carson 1998, 189).

King (1963) was dismayed by the clergy's concerns about the direct action and their lack of concern for the conditions that necessitated the demonstrations. While the clergy blamed King and others for inciting hatred and violence, King said "the city's white power structure left the Negro community with no alternative" (Carson 1998, 189). King went on to explain all of the efforts he and others took to negotiate with those in positions of power and their repeated unwillingness to operate in good faith (Carson 1998).

One of King's most important criticisms of the clergy group's concerns was regarding the timing of the demonstrations. Much like many of today's scholars, elected officials, and residents, including some black scholars and black elected officials, the clergy group did not find that direction action was politically feasible, or in King's words "well timed" (Carson 1998, 191). King's retort is much needed today. King said, "Frankly, I have yet to engage in a direct-action campaign that was 'well timed' in the view of those who have not suffered unduly from the disease of segregation" (Carson 1998, 191). What is unique about the present danger of promoting race-neutral policies and strategies in the face of the same types of social issues King sought to address in his letter and in the direct-action campaigns is that some people who have suffered from the consequences of racial injustices in America have joined the chorus of voices that sound very much like the group of eight Alabama rabbis, bishops, and reverends who wrote the original letter.

King made it plain as to why black people could not wait for a more politically feasible time. The following excerpt from his letter could be updated slightly to apply to the experiences of black people today. King was commenting how difficult it is for black people to wait,

> When you have seen vicious mobs lynch your mothers and fathers at will and drown your sisters and brothers at whim; when you have seen hate-filled policemen curse, kick, and even kill your black brothers and sisters; when you see the vast majority of your twenty million Negro brothers smothering in an airtight cage of poverty in the midst of an affluent society; when you suddenly find your tongue twisted and your speech stammering as you seek to explain to your six-year old daughter why she can't go to the public amusement park that has just been advertised on television, and see tears welling up in her eyes when she is told that Funtown is closed to colored children, and see ominous clouds of inferiority beginning to form in her little mental sky, and see her beginning to distort her personality by developing an unconscious bitterness toward white people when you have to concoct an answer for a five-year old son who is asking: Daddy, why do white people treat colored people so mean?"; when you take a cross-county drive and find it necessary to sleep night after night in the uncomfortable corners of your automobile because no motel will accept you; when you are humiliated day in and day out by nagging signs reading "white" and "colored"; when you first name becomes "nigger," your middle names becomes "boy" (however old you are), and your last name becomes "John," and your wife and mother are never given the respected title "Mrs."; when you are harried by day and haunted by night by the fact that you are a Negro, living constantly at tiptoe stance, never quite knowing what to expect next, and are plagued with inner fears and outer resentments; when you are forever fighting a degenerating sense of "nobodiness"—then you will understand why we find it difficult to wait. (Carson 1998, 192)

King (1963) was particularly concerned with the lack of support from the white church on the horrific experiences of black people in Birmingham and beyond. He found such white moderates, in many ways, as more dangerous than members of the White Citizen Council or the Ku Klux Klan (Carson 1998, 195). The white moderate who, included white church leaders, "paternalistically believes he can set the timetable for another man's freedom; who lives by a mythical concept of time and who constantly advises the Negro to wait for a 'more convenient season'" (Carson 1998, 195).

For King, time was neutral and not socially constructed (Carson 1998). White moderates mistakenly understood time "from the strangely irrational notion that there is something in the very flow of time that will inevitably cure all ills" (Carson 1998, 196). On the contrary, King claimed, "we must use time creatively, in the knowledge that the time is always ripe to do right" (Carson 1998, 196).

While King conceded that some white church leaders made sacrifices for the movement, their numbers were far fewer than he anticipated (Carson 1998). King expressed great disappointment in the white church and its leaders. Instead of being allies, "some have been outright opponents, refusing to understand the freedom movement and misrepresenting its leaders; all too many others have been cautious than courageous and have remained silent behind the anesthetizing security of stained-glass windows" (Carson 1998, 199). While the white church and its leadership could have used their capital to "reach the power structure," they did not (Carson 1998, 199–200). Furthermore, King described the white church as being complicit in the ongoing oppression of black people in the city. "Far from being disturbed by the presence of Church, the power structure of the average community is consoled by the Church's silent—and often even vocal—sanction of things as they are" (Carson 1998, 201). Such is the case today with white moderates, and even some black scholars and black elected officials as they give into white backlash and embrace race-neutral policies and programs as the relative inferior status of black people on a host of social and demographic outcomes remain at epidemic levels, such as in the case of the overrepresentation of black men in fatal police-involved shootings, black asset poverty, racial wealth inequality, and under resourced and disinvested schools and neighborhoods.

Based on this reading of King's work, and not just a cursory analysis of a few lines from his "I Have a Dream" speech, it is clear that not only was King not an interpreter or champion of, or for American civil religion, but one of its greatest critics. For King, American civil religion represented one of the greatest examples of the perversion of professed American values and ideals. This is particularly clear when King wrote, "the greatest blasphemy of the whole ugly process was that the white man ended up making God his partner in the exploitation of the Negro" (King 1967, 79). Indeed, King (1967) wrote, "white America has been backlashing on the fundamental God-given and human rights of Negro for more than three hundred years" (87).

More contemporarily, philosopher George Yancy has written about his experiences with white backlash. Yancy (2018) described the reactions of white people to a letter he published in 2015 in The Stone, the *New York Times*. The letter, which was published in the days leading to the Christmas holiday, was framed as a gift, as an offering of love. Yancy's intent was to assist white America in seeing their whiteness and the ways in which they benefit from the way American society is structured even when they think they are intentional about living in ways that are more tolerant and reflective. Yancy notes that just because people there are some white people who do not use racial slurs or openly support white nationalist groups doesn't mean they are not beneficiaries of racism and complicit in a variety of ways. Although Yancy anticipated some negative reactions to his letter, he did not anticipate the hatred filled white backlash he endured as a result of it. He was threatened with bodily harm, among other things. He had to alert campus police about threats. Yancy chose to expound about the backlash he experienced as a result of the 2015 letter and use it as an opportunity take a deeper dig into how racism functions and the roles that individuals and institutions play. Yancy's audience for the book is white Americans and his truth is the oppression and suffering of black people, as the metaphysical and paradigmatic other, historically and in contemporary times.

Stephen C. Finley, Biko Gray, and I also wrote about the backlash that black professors, like George Yancy, faced in response to comments they made on social media or in their classrooms during the course of doing what they were trained and hired to do (Finley et al. 2018). Scholars like Tommy Curry, Zandria Robinson, and Keeanga-Yamahtta Taylor were targeted by virtual mobs and in several cases, were abandoned by, or chastised by top administrators at their respective colleagues and universities. Other black professors have reported white backlash for statements they have made verbally or in writing. Some of these professors canceled invited lectures and other speaking engagements for their safety and the safety of their loved ones. The threat of white backlash is real and has serious consequences. Even when black scholars, and others, take calculated measures to minimize white backlash, they remain susceptible to all types of harm. Harkening back to Yancy's love gift to white America, we find that the noted philosopher attempted to soften the blow of his hard-hitting message by using himself as a model. In his letter, and later in his book, he describes himself as sexist and discusses all the ways that he tries to be intention about dismantling sexism but still finds himself complicit in the perpetuation of it and a beneficiary of his spoils. Yancy acknowledged that the experiences of black women, and other women of color, are unique to that of white women, but avoids delving into a complicated discussion about black men, black manhood, and white hegemonic patriarchy. Nonetheless, he uses himself as a model to deflect criticisms that he is placing a lot of blame on white America but, like many black people, fails to engage in a deep process of self-reflection. While Yancy's willingness to be open about his position in society as a man provides great insight, it also takes away from the main purpose of the letter, his book, and other brilliant publications he has authored on race. Even George Yancy, as brave and as honest a scholar that he is, has experienced what he calls the vitriol of white backlash and negotiates what he says and how he says it, which can have negative implications, including undermining the very message to white America he wanted to send. In effect, Yancy does not guide white America away from white innocence but lulls them further into a sense of security in it.

I have shown, as have others, that the King and the civil rights movement were far more complexed than some scholars and members of the general public tend to think. The civil rights and Black Power movements are still viewed by many as being on opposite ends of the social justice spectrum considering their respective preferred strategies. However, one thing they share that is understudied is the hope that the subordination of black people could change.

Ture and Hamilton (1992) wrote about fighting for black power. Ture clearly did not see the racial subordination of black people as permanent. Indeed, Ture and Hamilton (1992) argued that black people had to take care of their business or they would always remain subordinate to white people. The pair offered a framework, not a guidebook or blueprint, for attaining black power. Ture and Hamilton (1992) argued that black people would need to develop a sense of peoplehood. They would need to develop pride and not shame in their blackness. They conceded that race was not an easy topic to discuss. They found that both black and white people often found it embarrassing or inconvenient or confusing to discuss.

Ture and Hamilton (1992) highlighted the urgency of the challenges facing black people. They stated that there was no time to play nice because the very lives of little black boys and girls were at risk. Ture and Hamilton (1992) commented that "some white Americans can afford to speak softly, tread lightly, employ the soft-sell and put-off (or is it put-down?). They own the society. For black people to adopt their methods of relieving our oppression is ludicrous" (Ture and Hamilton 1992, xvii). It is clear here that Ture believes the conditions of black people can change and provides some direction for under what circumstances that can or cannot take place.

Ture embraced the language of black intellectual thinkers like Frederick Douglass over and above what he and Hamilton described as colorblind language, or empty words. For example, Ture and Hamilton (1992) quote

Douglass when he stated, "power concedes nothing without demand" (xvii). Additionally, they found power in the statement by Douglass that "the limits of tyrants are prescribed by the endurance of those whom they oppress" (Ture and Hamilton 1992, xviii).

Ture and Hamilton (1992) define racism as "the predication of decisions and policies on considerations of race for the purpose of subordinating a racial group and maintaining control over that group" (3). The authors describe individual and institutional racism. They describe individual racism as more overt than institutional racism. Institutional racism is akin to colonialism, argued Ture and Hamilton (1992). There is far less outcry in the case of institutional racism, according to Ture and Hamilton (1992). The doctrine of black inferiority and white superiority undergirds institutional racism. Ture and Hamilton (1992) argued black people were essentially a colony and that white people had no desire to set them free. The authors did offer a disclaimer. "This is not to say that every single white American consciously oppresses black people. He does not need to" (Ture and Hamilton 1992, 22). Ture and Hamilton (1992) further contended that colonialism both degraded and dehumanized black people.

Ture and Hamilton (1992) argued that black people had to redefine themselves. They needed to set new goals and organize around them. Ture and Hamilton (1992) identified the steps required for black people to achieve black power. The first step for Ture and Hamilton (1992) was for black people to develop a new consciousness or deniggerize. Ture and Hamilton (1992) also stated that black people needed a political modernization rooted in three major concepts. The major concepts included questioning old values and institutions, creating new and different political structures, and broadening political participation. Ture and Hamilton (1992) rejected assimilation into so-called middle-class America. They found middle-class American values to be anti-humanist and perpetuators of antiblack racism.

Ture and Hamilton (1992) understood the relatively disadvantaged position of black people in the United States but were convinced or duped into believing that the subordination of black people would change. They thought they had learned from the shortcomings of King's and other's nonviolent strategy and if they employed a new way of addressing racial injustices in the America that the outcome would be different. Ture and Hamilton (1992) called for black people to unite, recognize their heritage, and work toward building a greater sense of community. Black power, for Ture and Hamilton (1992), was built upon the premise that "before a group can enter the open society, it must first close ranks" (44). Again, Ture and Hamilton (1992), claimed that there were things that black people could do to change their subordinate status. Group solidarity, according to Ture and his co-author, was an option.

Moreover, Ture and Hamilton (1992) acknowledged that "the goal of the racists is to keep black people on the bottom," but firmly held that that would not always be the case, especially if black people adhered to the framework outlined in their book. The framework meant that black people who set aside certain language and no longer use terms like progress, nonviolent integration, fear of white backlash, or coalition. These words, according to Ture and Hamilton (1992), harmed the black struggle for liberation more than they aided the cause. For one, integration assumed the superiority of white people and the inferiority of black people. Coalitions often did not work because some so-called allies assumed that black people had the same interest as other reform groups. Ture and Hamilton (1992) contended that coalitions cannot exist between groups that are economically and politically secure and groups that are economically and politically insecure, such as black people. Finally, Ture and Hamilton (1992) warned that coalitions could not be sustained on a moral or friendly basis with polite appeals to an individual's or a group's conscience.

For Ture and Hamilton (1992) viable coalitions must be mutually beneficial and take into the various self-interests of each of the groups involved. They added that evidence of a black power base must be present before black people participate in a coalition. Ture and Hamilton (1992) identified four conditions that must be in place before black people partner with other activist groups. There must be an acknowledgment of self-interests. How black people benefit specifically from involvement in the coalition must be outlined. Each group must have an independent power base and the goals of the coalition must be specific and not general (Ture and Hamilton 1992).

To ensure that black people were not subordinate forever, Ture and Hamilton (1992) argued that black people had to organize themselves first. They critiqued white supporters who were willing to work with black people but not work within their own communities to end racism. Ture and Hamilton (1992) observed that "whenever black people have moved toward genuinely independent action; the society has distorted their intensions or damned their performance" (84).

Ture and Hamilton (1992) called for an independent politics and declared that an independent politics was essential to the liberation of black people. They concluded with a call for black people to be determined to "T.C.B.—take care of business. They will not be stopped in their drive to achieve dignity, to achieve their share of power, indeed, to become their own men and women—in this time and in this land—by whatever means necessary" (Ture and Hamilton 1992, 185). Ending the racial subordination of black people for Ture and others associated with the Black Power movement was possible and would require many to risk everything.

The Nation of Islam had a different view. While King and Ture placed great faith, hope, and trust, in the government and others, the Nation of Islam, particularly under the leadership of Minister Louis Farrakhan was less optimist and contended that the U.S. was a hypocritical nation with many leaders that could not be trusted and that the fate of the nation was doomed. Stephen C. Finely is one of the foremost experts on the NOI. In his article, "The Meaning of Mother in Louis Farrakhan's 'Mother Wheel,'" he discussed how central Farrakhan's experience was personally and to the group. Farrakhan described seeing what some might call an unidentified flying object (UFO). He was taken into the UFO where he say former leaders Master Fard Muhammad and the Honorable Elijah Muhammad. Both shared secret knowledge with Farrakhan and he and the organization were forever changed.

Finley (2012) stated that the Wheel, or the UFO in Farrakhan's encounter, "is encoded with the meaning of black bodies everywhere" (434). It was a form of a UFO counternarrative "created in order to survive in a hostile culture" (Finley 2012, 434). Moreover, Finley (2012) argued that the "purpose of creating new symbols and figures that one can then idealize" and create "the formation of healthy selves with regard to black people generally" (434–435). The significance of the Mother Wheel to "NOI thought and cosmology" should not be underestimated, argued Finley (2012, 436). The Wheel symbolized social and cosmic orders, according to Finley (2012).

While some have dismissed Farrakhan's 1955 and 1985 UFO accounts, they should be taken more seriously (Finley 2012). "UFOs are religious in the sense that they raise questions about the world (and the nature of the universe) and profound transformations of consciousness that have as a byproduct the reconstruction of mythologies that explain the world and give meaning and coherence to an otherwise absurd existence" (Finley 2012, 440). This is to say that UFOs provided the NOI and black people as a whole with a greater sense of self and "meaning beyond racist and narrow constructions of *black* as limited and inferior, and an accompanying alteration in consciousness that moves them to push against such contradictions (Finley 2012, 440).

The counternarratives subverted racism and extended the history and meaning of black people in America beyond the nation. This helped them to develop a "cosmic consciousness" to aid them in seeking justice (Finley 2012, 440). Finley (2012) further suggested that the Mother Wheel was understood to protect black people as they were God's chosen people. Moreover, the Mother Wheel represented "abstract conceptions such as truth, freedom, and purity" (Finley 2012, 448). It also served as a symbol of the "greatness and grandness of black intellect as well as technical superiority" (Finley 2011, 449). "The Mother Plane," another term used to describe the Mother Wheel, "would eventually bring peace on earth as well as retribution" (Finley 2013, 277). Hence, the NOI did not contend that the status of black people in

America was likely to change but developed ways "that allowed it to engage in a world in which its members felt marginalized and violated symbolically and actually . . . a sense of control over the meaning of 'black' bodies against a historical condition in which black bodies had been constructed by discursive and social practices that posited them as inferior" (Finley 2013, 259).

Farrakhan delivered a speech, "The Criterion," on July 4, 2020, which was the ninetieth anniversary of the NOI. His speech touched upon a number of topics including the coronavirus pandemic, the Trump administration, the Mother Wheel, and the killing of George Floyd. In what Farrakhan said might be his last speech, he made remarks that further support my contention that unlike King and Ture, Farrakhan and the NOI represented and continue to represent a departure from black leaders and predominately black-led movements in hoping that their actions and/or the benevolence of ordinary white citizens or the government will bring an end to the subordination of black people because of their racial classification. He described the loss of Brother Abdul Hafeez Muhammad, a minister in the East Coast Region, to the coronavirus and the loss of hundreds of thousands across the country. The stay-at-home orders provided Farrakhan with an opportunity to reflect on some important questions, he commented during the nearly three-hour long speech viewed by a small group in person and by thousands of people across the United States and around the world.

Farrakhan described a high-level of contemporary dissatisfaction with the way things were happening in the United States and in the world. He commented on his role as a messenger to help people not get caught up in what he described as the "folly of firecrackers and foolishness." He talked about the great white men who founded the United States and the words penned in the Declaration of Independence. He reminded those listening how many groups were not included in the new nation's promises, including black people. Farrakhan commented on the fact that for a time black people were considered three-fifths of a person. He acknowledged that the privileges outlined in the Constitution applied to white people who were considered deserving of privilege and no one else.

Farrakhan discussed the many years that black people were living in physical bondage. He connected it to what he described as the dog whistle in the call by President Donald Trump to Make America Great Again. Farrakhan interpreted the popular saying to mean, Make America White Again and stated that this meaning was driving white nationalists to Trump.

Farrakhan contrasted his response to the pandemic with that of Trump and his administration. Farrakhan reminded those in attendance to wear their masks and maintain social distancing. He cautioned them against becoming what he called "followers of the foolishness of our government." Farrakhan cited Trump's call to his supporters to push back against stay-at-home orders. Trump rallied them around calls for liberation. He rushed to open up society, claimed Farrakhan in an effort to increase his chances of remaining in power. This was evidenced by the return of professional basketball and church choirs, despite reports that some members of these groups tested positive for COVID-19, potentially spreading the deadly virus to others, argued Farrakhan.

In the speech Farrakhan stated that white people "were made to rule. White people wherever you find them on our planet; it doesn't make any difference where their entity or their ethnicity is, they are the same way by nature." Clearly, Farrakhan was not painting a picture whereby black people could do anything to change the racial status order in the United States, or anywhere else in the world. Agree or disagree with his claims about the "nature" of white people. What is clear was that he was not espousing the idea that anyone should expect the conditions of black people to change any time soon.

Farrakhan's distrust in the United States was further evidenced in his comments about a rush to produce a vaccine and test it on people in countries on the continent of Africa. He warned African leaders and called for a meeting that would include black "skilled virologists, epidemiologists, students or biology and chemistry and we need to look at not only what they give us, we need to give ourselves something better." Farrakhan added another word of warning. "When the White man was made his father was a liar, his father was a murderer, so they're born with life and murder in their nature. How do they lie so easily? If you could read the record, the police records of what they say in their reports that they write. They have concocted lies to justify their murder of our brothers and sisters." While King and Ture would join Farrakhan in condemning mistreatment by law enforcement officials against black people they would be more hopeful about their ability to change it where Farrakhan was making an argument that the racial status quo was permanent.

More than two hours into his speech, Farrakhan commented on the killing of George Floyd on May 25, 2020, and the so-called racial reckoning that was beginning in the country. Farrakhan stated that some white people, in an effort to appease black people, were willing to do things like take down depictions of Jesus as white. Farrakhan stated that these folks knew that Jesus was black and encouraged them to tell the truth about black Jesus. He described the killers of George Floyd and the terrible murder everyone was made to watch. Farrakhan described the officers as cowards and snakes and imaged that under other circumstances Floyd could have easily overcame them. Farrakhan described how peaceful Floyd was throughout much of the encounter that still ended with his death.

Floyd's death was a metaphor for the ongoing treatment of black people in America. Crying out in pain as Floyd did for his deceased mother and as individuals engaged in nonviolent strategies years ago did not change the outcome. Creating unity and a sense of group solidarity undoubtedly changed the messaging of certain companies, established new positions, and put a spotlight on issues of diversity, equity, and inclusion, but evidence on virtually all social outcomes shows the continued subordination of black people in America. While King and Ture were hopeful that the racial arrangement in America would change, Farrakhan and the NOI were convinced that it would not.

Farrakhan and the NOI's understanding of American history and what can be accomplished as far as black people were concerned is more in agreement with Bell's (1993) concept of racial realism than King or Ture. Indeed, Bell (1993) calls out the civil rights movement for what he considered an overreliance on courtroom victories and a belief in the racial neutrality of the law and of the justice system more broadly. Bell (1993) would agree with me that adherents to the civil rights movement were duped into thinking that they took a more moderate stance than other black people and worked through the legal system and that the humanity of black people would finally be acknowledged, and black people would also enjoy all the rights and privileges that other people had access to in the nation. Adherents to the Black Power movement were duped into thinking that if they were more forceful in their strategies then they could demand that the oppressors stop oppressing them and share power. The reality of the matter was that no matter what the adherents did on either side of the social justice spectrum or on any point in between that the racialized social system in America would remain unchanged; thus, black people would remain and continue to remain, as a group, a racially subordinated group.

In the next chapter, "Promises Unfulfilled: Black Lives Matter Chatter," I discuss #BlackLivesMatter—a popular hashtag that originated with the killing of Trayvon Martin in Sanford, Florida, by George Zimmerman. I discuss how it grew in popularity after the killing of George Floyd in Minneapolis, Minnesota, by several police officers. George Floyd's killing appeared to usher in a new or renewed interest in social justice issues. Colleges, universities, athletic teams, and corporations, among others, embraced the sentiments related to black lives matter. However, we can expect that many of these promises and actions will be short-lived given what we have seen on broader attacks on what many collectively refer to as affirmative action policies for black people. I discuss how colorblind ideology emerged as a response to affirmative action and that black people's faith that change had come was once again undermined. I draw upon racial realism to explain how and why this took place. Racial realism helps us to understand, I argue, why many of the efforts were more symbolic than substantive and why black people again have felt an enormous sense of disappointment in the promise of America.

## NOTE

1. Parts of this chapter were previously published in *America in Denial* (2021), Albany, NY: SUNY Press and are used with permission.

*Chapter Five*

# Promises Unfulfilled
## *Black Lives Matter Chatter*

Black people have been duped into thinking that America wants to do better. This has been evidenced by the push for affirmative action policies, support for the Black Lives Matter Movement, and for greater awareness about diversity, equity, and inclusion issues following the killing of George Floyd in Minneapolis, Minnesota, as well as the killing of other unarmed black men and women at the hands of white police officers and ordinary citizens. In this chapter, I begin with the history of affirmative action and then the related backlash. I then discuss the origins and growth of the Black Lives Matter Movement. Next, I discuss how some individuals and groups responded to the brutal killing of George Floyd and the evidence that already suggests that far too many black people and well-meaning white people got their hopes up that America was forever changed only to see mounting evidence of the continued significance of race. I conclude the chapter by demonstrating how Bell's (1993) concept of racial realism helps us understand the subject matters covered.

## A BRIEF HISTORY OF AFFIRMATIVE ACTION IN AMERICA

Many Americans think they know what affirmative action is and is not. However, like many other terms in the American lexicon, the term has been used and altered from its intended meaning to meet the agendas and interests of various individuals and groups. The University of Rhode Island provided an important history about affirmative action, which for the institution, begins in 1961. On March 6, 1961, President John F. Kennedy issued Executive Order 10925. The order created the Committee on Equal Employment Opportunity. The Committee included the Vice President, Secretary of Labor,

Secretary of Defense, and the Secretaries of the Army, Navy, and Air Force, among others. The purpose of the order and the Committee was to make sure that hiring and employment practices were free from racial discrimination.

In Executive Order 10925, Kennedy made several statements. He stated that racial discrimination was contrary to the principles of the Constitution. He said that the U.S. government was obligated to make sure that equal opportunities existed for all qualified individuals. Kennedy encouraged the use of positive measures that would lead to greater opportunities. He contended that doing so was in the interest of the nation. Kennedy described the need for such action as urgent.

In the order, Kennedy called for an end to racial discrimination in all government employment. He directed all Executive Departments and agencies to conduct studies of their employment practices. He outlined the obligations also for government contractors and subcontractors. Any contractor or subcontractor found discriminating on the bases of race may find themselves ineligible to do business with the U.S. government in the future. Executive Order 10925 also included sanctions and penalties for non-compliance, including criminal proceedings and the publishing of the names of violators.

The University of Rhode Island also pointed to the historic Civil Rights Act of 1964 as an important point in the history of affirmative action in America. The act prohibited racial discrimination in all areas of public accommodation. Shortly after the signing of the Civil Rights Act of 1964, President Lyndon B. Johnson spoke on the occasion of the Howard University commencement. On June 4, 1965, he talked about the meaning of freedom. He described freedom as the right to be treated as a person equal with the promise and dignity in all areas of life. Johnson went on to say that being free was simply not enough. President Johnson said gates of opportunity must be opened but black people must be able to walk through them. Johnson commented, "We seek not just freedom but opportunity." He added that we seek equality both as a fact and a result.

The issuance of Executive Order 11246 enforced affirmative action. The order required agencies to take specific measures to ensure equality in hiring to documentation of said efforts. The 1969 Philadelphia Order, issued by President Richard Nixon, was another important moment in the history of Affirmative Action in America, according to the University of Rhode Island. The order guaranteed fair hiring practices in the construction industry. The University of Rhode Island document commented that craft unions were among the greatest offenders with respect to racial discrimination in hiring. The order required the industry to set goals and timetables. It urged them to show affirmative action. It did not require quotas but tried to increase non-white employment.

One of the most historic affirmative action cases in the history of America was the *Bakke* case, which took place in June 1978. A white applicant to the University of California Medical School claimed he was denied admission while lesser qualified nonwhite students were accepted. The case severely limited affirmative action. *Bakke* claimed he experienced reverse discrimination because the Medical School reserved 16 of 100 places for minority and economically disadvantaged students. *Bakke* successfully argued that the admissions policy violated the Equal Protection Clause of the Fourteenth Amendment. The U.S. Supreme Court ruled that colleges and universities could not use inflexible quotas.

In *Wygant v. Jackson Board of Education*, in May 1986, litigants challenged a policy that laid off non-minorities first. Almost a year later in *U.S. v. Paradise,* the State of Alabama Department of Public Safety was ordered to institute specific racial quotas because the department failed to comply with other orders to end their racially discriminatory practices. The Court upheld the use of strict quotas in the case. By January 1989, in *City of Richmond v. Croson,* the courts were deciding whether set asides for black-owned firms were lawful. The Court ruled that there must be evidence of widespread racial discrimination in an industry, according to the University of Rhode Island's Affirmative Action History. And yet on June 12, 1995, in *Adarand Constructors, Inc. v. Pena,* the court supported race-specific remedial measures in selected cases.

That same year, the Clinton administration offered some mixed messaging regarding affirmative action. Clinton stated that the *Adarand* case highlighted the need for affirmative action, but Clinton also called for an end to any programs that included quotas, hired unqualified people, led to reverse discrimination, or continued after racial discrimination ended.

In *Hopwood v. University of Texas,* in March 1996, the court disagreed with the argument that diversity was a legitimate goal for colleges and universities. Ensuring a diverse student body was not, according to the courts, a compelling state interest. The court encouraged race-neutral criteria for admissions.

Shortly thereafter states began introducing propositions to ban affirmative action. According to the University of Rhode Island timeline, California banned all affirmative action in 1997. About a year later, Washington became the second state to ban affirmative action with Initiative 200.

By February 2000, Florida declared that race could not be a factor in college admissions. Later that year in *Gratz v. Bollinger,* the courts declared that the use of race was constitutional in college admissions and that a diverse study body was indeed a compelling interest. The court also noted here that other groups receive preferences, such as in the case of the children of alumni and athletes. In a similar case, both involving the University of Michigan, in

*Gutter v. Bollinger*, the course concluded the opposite and was reversed on appeal in 2002.

In June 2003, the U.S. Supreme Court upheld affirmative action in university admissions. The University of Rhode Island described the decision as the most important since the *Bakke* decision. The Court found that a diverse student body was important. Three years later, the Court ruled against considering race to integrate schools and this ruling was viewed as a setback to affirmative action.

Nebraska and Colorado also considered banning affirmative action in 2008. The bans were rejected in both states. But about seven months later, a group of white firefighters in New Haven, Connecticut, filed a lawsuit, *Ricci v. DeStefano,* claiming reverse discrimination when the results for exams for leadership positions were thrown out when the results showed that few nonwhites met the threshold to become lieutenants or captains.

The most recent case included on the timeline was *Fisher v. University of Texas.* In this case, the Court ruled that universities could consider race to achieve diversity but that they had to try other non-race-specific strategies as well. The University of Rhode Island described the decision as a compromise between liberal and conservative members of the Court.

Margaret Kramer also provided a useful timeline of the history of affirmative action but focused entirely on college admissions. Karmer (2019) discussed *Bakke, Bollinger, and Fischer,* but also included *Marco DeFunis, Jr. v. University of Washington Law School.* In this 1974 case, DeFunis, a white man, claimed he was denied admissions into the University of Washington Law School while less qualified nonwhite students were admitted. He gained admissions and eventually graduated (Karamer 2019). The case was the first since the 1960s.

The variations in the legal decisions about affirmative action as well as public opinion were rooted in many myths about black people and about programs that were established to redress past racial wrongs. The University of Rhode Island identified four popular myths. First, many white Americans, including many white jurists, equate affirmative action with quotas. Second, many white Americans view affirmative action as reverse discrimination. Racial discrimination was meant to disadvantage black people and providing black people with opportunities to advance somehow disadvantages and discriminates against white people. Discrimination against black people can be tolerated but perceived discrimination against white people must end immediately. Another myth was that affirmative action rewards race and not achievement. Finally, the fourth myth about affirmative action was that there was a small pool of qualified black candidates, hence, their underrepresentation.

In reality, affirmative action programs often include targets and operate on good faith and may include specific benchmarks in the most overt cases of racial discrimination. Additionally, black people remain underrepresented and relatively disadvantaged relatively to white people in virtually every industry that reverse discrimination exists and/or was widespread is not supported by the facts. Third, affirmative action programs ensured that only the most qualified applicants were hired, and evidence has shown that black applicants often have to be more qualified than nonblack people applying for the same position to even get noticed, let alone hired. Finally, there were claims that there were only a small number of qualified black people in any industry when one of the real issues was the lack of recruitment efforts to potential black candidates, according to the University of Rhode Island's Myths and Reality document about affirmative action.

Perhaps if more people understood the origins of the term they would have a better understanding of how it was intended to work. Jackie Mansky wrote about the origins of the term in a 2016 article. Marksky (2016) observed that the term appeared in the 1935 National Labor Relations Act, also known as the Wagner Act. The Act encouraged active measures to treat employees fairly. The Act established the National Labor Relations Board and ushered in collective bargaining. It addressed discriminatory labor practices but did not specifically take up the issue of race. Mansky (2016) added that it was President Roosevelt's Executive Order 8802, issued in 1941, that addressed fair employment practices and considered race in response to a threatened march on Washington by black labor leader, A. Phillip Randolph. Roosevelt did not use the phrase affirmative action in the order. The march was eventually called off but just a few years later, Mansky (2016) argued that "industrial intolerance remained deep-rooted."

President Eisenhower followed with Executive Order 10479 in 1953. The order addressed antidiscrimination and created the Committee on Government Contracts. President Kennedy as noted previously was the first to use the phrase affirmative action. Mansky (2016) added that the concept of affirmative action was expanded to include education later and was received with enormous levels of resistance as evidenced in the *Bakke* case discussed previously.

President Obama added sexual orientation and gender in 2014 to Johnson's Executive Order 11246 (Mansky 2016).

Jacqueline Yi and Nathan Todd (2021) found that there was a relationship between opposition to affirmative action, legitimizing ideologies, and anti-blackness. Legitimizing ideologies to "maintain that society is fair primarily by holding individuals solely responsible for their outcomes and social standing, rather than attributing unequal relationships among groups to systemic inequality" (Yi and Todd 2021, 2).

Some Americans, especially black Americans, had hoped that legitimizing ideologies would be a thing of the past in the wake of far too many to name black men, women, and children killed by white police officers and ordinary white citizens. The hashtag, #BlackLivesMatter, was born out of a desire for white people in America to finally see the humanity of black people. After the killing of barely seventeen-year-old Trayvon Martin by George Zimmerman in Sanford, Florida, the hashtag emerged. Martin was killed by Zimmerman in part because the latter thought the former looked suspicious and was out of place. Martin, a young black male, was simply enjoying the NBA All-Star weekend and returning from purchasing some snacks when an encounter with Zimmerman ended his life. Zimmerman was not immediately charged and when he finally went to trial, he was found not guilty. Three queer-identifying black women were credited with originating the hashtag. The use of the hashtag and statement grew with the killing of Michael Brown in Ferguson, Missouri. Brown was also not armed, reportedly raised his hands to demonstrate so, and was killed by police. His body lay in the street for hours. His death led to the collective outcry, "Hands Up! Don't Shoot."

The movement and phrase gained new life after the killing of George Floyd, and in that it was shown and voiced by groups and individuals that remained relatively silent in the past, including professional sports teams, legal associations, major corporations, and even colleges and universities. While many were applauded for commenting on such a horrific display and disregard for human life, many were also critiqued for not taking a strong enough stance.

Judy Perry Martinez, President of the American Bar Association, issued a statement in 2020. She said she was saddened and expressed concern about violence against people of color. She noted that the overwhelming majority of protestors were peaceful and that most in law enforcement were fair and just people of integrity. Martinez did not speak to the violence against black people specifically and appeared to craft her statement to say as President Trump has said in the past that there are good and bad on both sides. Martinez did not make one specific reference to George Floyd in the statement.

There was a statement by the Minnesota State Bar Association and other groups described the "violent killing of George Floyd." The group also said they joined "in the grief and anger." They vowed to honor Floyd's death and promised he would not be forgotten. They expressed a commitment to bring justice for Floyd, his family, and the broader community. The state bar association acknowledged that Floyd's death was not an isolated incident but part of a larger ongoing problem. They added that no one should feel safe when something like what happen to Floyd occurs. The Minnesota State Bar Association and cosigners vowed to confront systems and cultures in police departments that allowed people of color to be brutalized and killed. They hoped for a state where no one would fear the police and the use of force would be a last resort and not the first choice. They mentioned the need to build trust and hoped for healing. The groups concluded their statements with a commitment to continue working for equal justice. The Minnesota State Bar Association led statement represented an improvement from national association's statement in that it addressed Floyd specifically and called out the systemic problems, but the use of the term "people of color" in the statement masks the antiblackness at the center of Floyd's killing and the killing of so many other black people in the country.

Professional athletic leagues also issued statements after the killing of George Floyd. While it was not uncommon for individual athletes to speak out on racial injustices, such as in the case of Tommie Smith, John Carlos, and Colin Kaepernick, or for teams, such as in the case of the Miami Heat, after the killing of Trayvon Martin, it has not always been the case that entire leagues have rallied behind such causes. Indeed, the National Basketball Association (NBA), had the phrase, Black Lives Matter, prominently placed on many of the courts and teams wore game jerseys with social justice messages. The response was in sharp contrast to the reactions of leagues like the National Football League (NFL) after Kaepernick and others protested during the customary playing of the national anthem at the start of each game. Criticisms of Kaepernick came from many sources, including other players, fans, owners, and then President Donald Trump.

Adam Silver, NBA Commissioner, sent a memorandum to all the league employees and in it expressed outrage for the killings of Floyd and others, including Breonna Taylor. He expressed his outrage and offered condolences. He used the "R" word. Silver commented, "Racism, police brutality, and racial injustice remain part of everyday life in America and cannot be ignored." He promised to promote inclusion and work to bridge divides. He called for "collective action, civic engagement, candid dialogue" and offered "support for organizations working towards justice and equality." The NBA is comprised of a majority of black players but continues to struggle with racial inequities, such as in the underrepresentation of black people in decision-making positions.

Many college and university administrators also issued statements following the killing of George Floyd. Lindsay McKenzie (2020) described some of the statements. McKenzie (2020) highlighted some that fell short and offered recommendations for what an effective statement should include, thanks to an interview with scholar Shaun Harper.

McKenzie (2020) observed that many statements from college and university administrators spoke out against racism and police brutality and included commitments to diversity, equity, and inclusion. However, far too few of the statements mentioned black people, Black Lives Matter, or actionable items.

It is important to note also that calls for institutional changed preceded the killing of George Floyd and many of the calls were not acted upon. At a minimum, the statements should have expressed empathy and solidarity with the Floyd family and the broader black community. Some of the statements issued by colleges and universities received very public negative feedback causing some administrators to issue revised statements. This was the case at Brown University and Christopher Newport University. Comments from Shaun Harper highlighted what the statements should have included. Harper said administrators should name antiblackness and admit the killing of black people by police. He argued that the aftermath of the killing of George Floyd was not the time for an all-lives matter approach. The phrase All-Lives Matter was used mainly by some white Americans to critique the statement Black Lives Matter as if the latter was elevating the lives of black people over the lives of others.

Harper also told McKenzie (2020) that colleges and universities should avoid general commitments to diversity, equity, and inclusion. They should directly identify and address white supremacy and antiblackness. Performative acts, commented Harper, were not acceptable. College and university administrators should issue statements because they believe they were warranted not because others were doing so. Harper urged colleges and universities to listen to black voices and not rely on advice from communication specialists where black people were often underrepresented or nonexistent. Harper also appealed to college and university administrators to take some political risks. He called for the hiring of more black administrators and black faculty. He asked that colleges and universities give more support to black studies programs and investigate campus police. In short, Harper called upon colleges and universities to "actualize Black Lives Matter," and not simply say it.

Andrew Elfenbein, Professor and Chair, of the Department of English at the University of Minnesota seemed to incorporate much of what McKenzie (2020) and Harper stated in his revised statement. Elfenbein acknowledged that the published statement was revised after several students took issue with the contents. Elfenbein's colleagues wanted it to be known that he was not speaking for the department or for other faculty and he stated as much in the beginning of the document. Elfenbein opened the statement with the phrase Black Lives Matter. He described Floyd's death and racial and economic injustices, more generally, as injustices. He said there was a need to foster anti-racism. He mentioned that the department developed diversity, equity, and inclusion goals that were available on their website and that the department would regularly monitor progress toward the goals. He expressed a commitment to social justice.

Elfenbein noted the power of language and described how terms like rioters and looters that were found in some statements were used to discredit black activism. He wanted to give space to black voices and included a statement from Terrion Williamson of the African American and African Studies Department. In that statement, Williamson addressed policing as a form of social control and the effects of racists logics on policing. Williamson linked Floyd's death to the pandemic and its disproportionate effects on black communities.

Williamson commented on the ways in which places in the Midwest were often characterized and racialized. Williamson paints a vivid picture of the different lived experiences of black and white people in the region. For example, Williamson noted in their statement that the Twin Cities, Minneapolis and Saint Paul, were ranked as the sixth Best Places in the United States at the same time that they were ranked fourth on the list of the Worst Cities for Black Americans.

Elfenbein again engaged with readers after including Williamson's statement and declared that it was not up to black people to enact anti-racist reform. He added that there was a need to change structures and acknowledged that the department had more to do. Elfenbein advocated for black-led social justice organization, including those working to end police violence and then provided a list of relevant resources. Elfenbein's statement was stronger because he listed to the voices and relied on the expertise of black people in his network.

Statements issued by colleges and universities have provided some hope to black students, faculty, staff, and communities that a period of racial reckoning was among us but there is evidence that was not the case. Evidence that the country is still not ready to treat black people with the humanity and dignity they deserve was evident support for Dereck Chauvin, the former officer who was convicted of killing George Floyd. It is also shown in the so-called fight against Critical Race Theory.

Many black Americans never thought they would see the day when a white officer would be charged with killing a black person let alone be sentenced to 270 months in prison but that was the decision handed down to Chauvin by Peter Cahill, Judge of the District Court, filed on June 25, 2021. Chauvin was found guilty by a jury on April 20, 2021, of "Count I, unintentional second-degree murder while committing a felony, third-degree murder, perpetrating an eminently dangerous act evincing a depraved mind, and Count II, second-degree manslaughter, culpable negligence creating an unreasonable risk" (1). There was much to celebrate about his conviction and sentencing but a careful reading of the sentencing order and memorandum opinion shows that black America has been duped if they are to think that this conviction and sentencing signifies an end to their racial subordination in America.

In the sentencing order and memorandum opinion, the judge announced his sentence and then explained how he arrived at the sentence. Floyd's family and the State of Minnesota had asked for a longer sentence. Unsurprisingly, Chauvin and his attorneys wanted the judge to use his discretion and depart from the presumptive sentencing guidelines. The document notes that "The Minnesota Sentencing Guidelines were promulgated 'to establish rational and consistent sentencing standards that promote public safety, reduce sentencing disparity, and ensure that the sanction imposed are proportional to the severity of the . . . offense and the offender's criminal history'" (Cahill 2021). District courts may, according to Judge Cahill, offer more or less time depending on the extent to which the crime was "'more or less serious than that typically involved in the commission of the crime in question'" (Cahill 2021). Chauvin was facing between 128 and 180 months in accordance with the guidelines. Cahill (2021) noted that consideration outside the guidelines involved two stages. "In the first stage, either a jury or the district court must make a factual finding that there are one or more aggravating factors present in the commission of the crime apart from the prima facie elements of the charged crime. In the second stage, the district court is required to explain why the presence of any such aggravating factors creates a substantial and compelling reason to impose a sentence outside the presumptive guidelines range" (Cahill 2021, 4).

The State presented five aggravated sentencing factors during the trial. The Court's verdict found support for four aggravated factors. The four factors included the finding that Chauvin abused his position; treated Floyd with cruelty; committed the crime in front of minor persons; and committed the crime as a part of a group. Cahill (2021) had to decide "whether any of these four aggravated factors demonstrated the Mr. Chauvin's conduct in connection with the offense for which he has been convicted renders his conduct significantly more serious than that typically involved in the commission of such an offense" (5).

Chauvin and his attorneys wanted a probationary sentence. Chauvin was the architect of a summer of racial reckoning because of his total disregard for George Floyd's personhood and everyone saw it and he still had the audacity to claim that he was just doing his job and should not serve any time in prison. The judge wisely found that "a probationary sentence would be disproportionate and understate the severity of Mr. Chauvin's offense" (Cahill 2021, 6). Chauvin maintained that "'he was simply performing his lawful duty in assisting other offers in the arrest of George Floyd . . . and was action 'in good faith reliance [on] his own experience as a police officer and the training he had received'" (Cahill 2021, 6). Chauvin's claim was rejected by all officers testifying during the trial (Cahill 2021).

Judge Cahill found support for the argument that Chauvin abused his position of trust and authority. The relationship between Chauvin and Floyd even though they did not know each other prior to the killing was "fraught with power imbalances that may make it difficult for a victim to protect himself"

(Cahill 2021, 7). The "unreasonable force" Chauvin used to hold Floyd faced-down on the street while in handcuffs was one example (Cahill 2021, 7). The duration of the assault on Floyd, which lasted over nine minutes, was also noted. Cahill (2021) added, "That 'failure to render aid became particularly abusive after Mr. Floyd had passed out, and was still being restrained in the prone position, with Mr. Chauvin continuing to kneel on the back of Mr. Floyd's neck with one knee and on his back with another knee, for more than two and a half minutes after one of his fellow officers announced he was unable to detect a pulse'" (Cahill 2021, 8).

Judge Cahill (2021) found merit in the State's claim that Chauvin's treatment of Floyd was particularly cruel and thus an aggravating factor. The document points to "'gratuitous infliction of pain,' and 'psychological cruelty'" (Cahill 2021, 11). Chauvin, the judge agreed, "killed Mr. Floyd 'slowly'" (Cahill 2021, 14). Judge Cahill (2021) did not consider the fourth factor involving Chauvin's participation as a member of a group. Cahill (2021) stated that given the findings on two of the four factors that "the Court need not wade into the morass of conflicting laws on this issue and come to a definitive conclusion. In short, the Court bases its decision to depart without regard to this factor" (Cahill 2021, 19). The issue Cahill (2021) referred to involved whether the participating officers could be considered offenders or not since none of the other officers have been convicted.

Where some might take issue with the sentencing and explanation was with the factor related to the commission of a crime in the presence of children. "The Court concludes the presence of that factor does not, under all the facts and circumstances of this case, present a substantial and compelling reason for an upward durational departure" (Cahill 2021, 16). Judge Cahill elaborated on how he arrived at the decision. He described three of the children as "young women" (Cahill 2021, 16). For most people, the three young females were girls or minors. Cahill (2021) also acknowledged the presence of a nine-year-old girl. Cahill (2021) commented that "none was a victim in the sense of being physically injured or threatened with Mr. Chauvin and his co-defendant officers" (16). Cahill (2021) added that they "were never coerced or forced by him or any of the other officers to remain a captive presence at the scene and did not known any or the officers or Mr. Floyd" (16).

Judge Cahill's assessment of the harm caused by witnessing the killing of George Floyd was indicative of a broader failure on the part of many white people in America to see black youth as children. Many fail to see the innocence and vulnerability in black youth that they readily see in their own children, family members, neighbors, and friends. Cahill (2021) made no mention of the psychological harm or the fact that one of more of the black youth watching the horrific killing may have been paralyzed with fear or were fearful that they might be harmed if they attempted to do anything, including leave the scene. In fact, Cahill (2021) noted that one or more of the youth was observed smiling and sometimes laughing on the video of Floyd's death. Cahill (2021) like far too many white Americans was normalizing black death. The underlying assumption was that black youth routinely experience violence and thus were not harmed here and no one should be held accountable. At the same time, the presence of black youth may be used to enhance sentences when the defendant is black but when the defendant is white, it is not even taken into account.

At the same time that black and white Americans were breathing a sigh of relief that Chauvin was not only convicted but sentenced for his crime, a battle was continuing to rage on about the place of race in the history of American education. Debates about critical race theory, for example, are not new but were usually relegated to articles and books about the framework written by informed scholars and not used as a lightning rod to attract angry white men and women who felt threatened by black progress and a sense of responsibility and blame for the nation's racist past.

In the popular press and to uninformed members of the general public, including some scholars at American colleges and universities, Critical Race Theory is a dirty three letter phrase that seeks to rewrite American history and to prohibit teachers and professors from teaching about racism and the legacies of slavery are currently being seriously considered in many states. How could it be that less than a year after the killing of George Floyd and only months after the United States named Juneteenth a national holiday could white Americans be celebrating the Fourth of July and questioning the patriotism of black people who refuse to celebrate a holiday that celebrates freedom, while many of their ancestors were still in physical bondage? How could so many black woman athletes in sports from across the Olympic spectrum face so many barriers and obstacles in their quest for gold particularly when they are relatively underrepresented numerically by shining among the most decorated?

Derrick Bell's racial realism provides us with a framework for understanding the enduring racial divides that have characterized this nation for its 245 years of existence and even before that time. The United States has not in the past and is not now interested in seeing nonwhite Americans as equals. The nation acts only when compelled to, for example, to avoid embarrassment on the world stage when chastising other nations about human, civil, and civil violations. As Bell noted, it is only when the interests of white American converge with the suffering of black people that peaks of progress occur. Understanding the permanent racial subordination of black people in America is powerful in making sense of how a nation and its citizens can claim to embrace diversity and at the same time work to undermine efforts at creating a more just and equitable nation that includes respecting the dignity and humanity of black people in all areas of society.

Black people have had their hopes built up more times than they care to admit only to realize that they had been duped or tricked into believing that America really meant what it said that they were equal and entitled to life, liberty, and the pursuit of happiness. They could ride in the front of buses, attend integrated schools, play on integrated sports teams, and yet that also meant that they would continue to be lynched, disproportionately harmed by police brutality, have relatively low or no levels of wealth, and live their lives under a constant cloud of white suspicion. There are some black people who apparently are easily duped and continue to have high hopes that the racial subordination of black people will change and then there are a small few who agree with Bell that the subordinate status of black people is permanent and have committed their lives works to exposing this reality and finding power in the fight. I count myself among the later.

# Conclusion
## *Racism, COVID-19, and Election 2020*

I end the book here with my thoughts on racial realism and understanding the effects of COVID-19 on black people and reactions to the attack on the U.S. Capitol on January 6, 2021.[1] At of the time of this writing, the COVID-19 pandemic is not over but America has started the process of opening up again. Hundreds of thousands of Americans have died in the global pandemic. In some places, black communities have been hardest hit. The effects of the insurrection at the Capitol are still being felt. First, we turn our attention to racism and the COVID-19 pandemic in the U.S.

### BLACK DEATHS AND COVID-19

A report from APM Research Lab includes data on COVID-19 deaths by race in America. More than 170,000 people died from COVID-19, as of August 18, 2020. The race and ethnicity for all but 5 percent is known, according to APM Research Lab. There were 88.4 black deaths per 100,000 people compared to 54.4 white deaths per 100,000 people during the same time. "Black Americans continue to experience the highest actual COVID-19 mortality rates nationwide—more than twice as high for Whites and Asians, who have the lowest actual rates" (APM Research Lab 2020).

Rayshawn Ray was among the scholars to take a deeper dive and focus on specific places where black people were overrepresented among COVID-19 deaths. Ray (2020) also explored why black people were dying at higher rates of COVID-19. Ray (2020) observed that in the State of Illinois, black people made up about 16 percent of the population but one-third of people diagnosed with COVID-19. In the city of Chicago, 70 percent of the people who died of COVID-19 were black. Ray (2020) observed that similar patterns were evidenced in states like New York and the Carolinas. In Louisiana, about 30 percent of the population identified as black. Seventy percent of COVID-19 deaths in Louisiana were black deaths.

Although some have argued that racial disparities in the prevalence of pre-existing health conditions explains the overrepresentation of black people among COVID-19 deaths, Ray (2020) contended that structural conditions that are related to pre-existing conditions and health disparities were more to blame. Ray (2020) pointed to the linkages between the racial composition of neighborhoods and health outcomes and the role that public policies played in creating under resourced black neighborhoods, such as the policy of redlining (Martin 2019). Redlining identified predominately black neighborhoods as hazardous and poor places for financial investment from mainstream lenders, including the federal government (Massey and Denton 1993). Black neighborhoods often have a higher population density than other neighborhoods making physical distancing to flatten the curve in their communities more challenging (Massey and Denton 1993). Access to testing, pharmacies, and health care professionals were issues prior to COVID-19, but factors that nevertheless served as structural barriers that contributed to the overrepresentation of black people among COVID-19 deaths (Ray 2020). Environmental racism and the criminalization of black men may also explain COVID-19 deaths among black people in America. Black people across the U.S. have faced greater environmental threats than other groups. Ray (2020) cites the toxic water in Flint, Michigan and the high levels of lead exposure in black communities in Baltimore. Finally, Ray (2020) argued that wearing personal protective equipment (PPE), like masks, is interpreted differently based upon race and gender, which may have served as a deterrent for some black men, for example, to embrace wearing a mask prior to statewide mandates. Historically, the dominant narrative about black men in America includes characterizations of the group as violent and a threat to white people and the society more broadly (Fashing-Varner et al. 2014).

Continuing efforts to trick black people into believing that the nation truly cares about them is killing them figuratively and literally. Black people are routinely reminded of who and what is valued in American society. One need only look at the responses to the stay-at-home orders by many white men, including in the Midwest and how law enforcement dealt with them when compared to the treatment of protestors identified with the Black Lives Matter movement. In my book, *America in Denial*, I wrote the following about what I described as a sixth trial in the history of American civil religion (Martin 2021).

I wrote that a sixth trial has emerged due to the COVID-19 global pandemic and the key word here is liberation. Much like the previous trials, there is a perception among members of the dominant racial group in America, most visibly, white men in America, that they are being victimized. Policies aimed at "flattening the curve" have been framed by white men from the president to several of his advisors to members of the Republican party, particularly in states led by democratic governors, as infringing upon *their* rights. Direct and implied calls for white men to protect and exert their rights, namely those afforded by the First and Second Amendments, are troubling, but not surprising when understood within the context of American civil religion. The contemporary response to the perceived attack on America, read as white America, by way of state and federal stay-at-home orders aimed at slowing the spread of the COVID-19 global pandemic, was religious and American civil religion is powerful analytical tool for informing the sociology of religion and public discourses about the roles of race and religion in society, including American civil religion.

The perceived inherent pathology of nonwhite bodies, especially black bodies, has resulted in the past as a failure to adequately respond to a social challenge. For example, sickle cell anemia impacts people of all races, but is considered colloquially as a black disease (Ciribassi and Patil 2016) and has not received the attention and support that other diseases have received by way of a federal response over many administrations. Many have compared the response to the crack epidemic and the ongoing opioid epidemic. The former, which disproportionately impacted black people, resulted in the further criminalizing of an entire group of people, while the latter, which disproportionately impacts white people, was medicalized and showered with federal resources ("A Tale of Two Epidemics" n.d.).

The preference shown to white bodies and matters impacting white people emboldens commonly held myths and stereotypes that are at the core of American civil religion and whiteness. Long before Theodore Roosevelt and the Rough Riders, there was a perception about the linkages between the body, the nation, and religion. Concepts such as Christian masculinity and muscular assimilation are noteworthy here (Martin 2017). This is to say that despite the numbers and what is still not known about COVID-19, some members of the dominant group believe that they are at greater risk of losing their rights as citizens than contacting COVID-19 and view "social distancing" strategies imminent threats.

The myth that COVID-19 or any other tragedy or trauma of the magnitude of a Hurricane Katrina or a COVID-19 pandemic does not discriminate is simply not true. However, myths and misrepresentations have their place American civil religion and are key for explaining white responses in such moments. Their perceived victimization lies in a strong adherence to American civil religion and their perceived supremacy as both white individuals and as a nation.

During what I am calling a sixth trial, many members of the dominant group struggled to come to terms with the differences between how America, especially white America, sees itself and the reality of how America actually works. Many experienced *white religious shock*, a disorientation based upon their racial position as it became painfully clear that the nation was ill-prepared to deal with an issue of this magnitude. It was unfathomable, for many, for example, how a nation that has long viewed itself as the savior of the world, did not have enough basic PPE for health care officials or first responders, who are often worshiped as heroes or treated as gods. It was likely incomprehensible to many that the nation lacked an adequate number of ventilators to support patients in need. The nation with the world's best and brightest had no reliable means of curing people of COVID-19 or vaccinating people against it was hard for some to grasp.

Without an effective way to test people for COVID-19 and no reliable cures available, many states announced disaster declarations and a national emergency, mentioned previously, was declared. A patchwork of plans meant that some states had very strict policies relative to others and for a time, some states had no plans at all. According to the *New York Times*, by early April 2020 at least 300 million people in about forty states were urged to stay at home. Washington D.C., for example, issued a stay-at-home order on March 30, 2020. Mayor Muriel Bowser said staying at home was the best way to "flatten the curve." Residents were instructed not to leave their homes unless they were engaged in essential activities, such as for medical appointments, buying food, performing or accessing essential governmental functions, and working at essential businesses. Failure to comply with the order could result in a fine of up to $5,000, imprisonment up to ninety days, or both.

In New York, non-essential businesses were closed as of March 22, 2020. Non-essential gatherings of individuals of any size for any reason were prohibited. Residents were asked to stay no less than six feet from another. Limitations were also placed on outdoor recreational activities. The maximum fine for violators was $1,000.

In Louisiana, as of March 11, 2020, nonessential businesses were to close. Residents were asked to exercise proper social distancing in public and all gatherings of ten people or more were prohibited. The order outlined examples of essential activities. No fines or imprisonment were mentioned.

Michigan announced a stay-at-home order that went into effect on March 24, 2020. Michigan's order prohibited nonessential in-person work and called for social distancing. Violation of the order was described as a misdemeanor.

Public service announcements featuring the Chief Executive Officers of major corporations, college football coaches, entertainers, local elected officials, and others encouraged people to do their part to mitigate the threat of COVID-19 by obeying the orders and staying home. While some people viewed the orders as are necessary, others viewed it as a threat.

Media accounts of largely white people protesting in states, such as Michigan, are framed as protests against social distancing orders. *HuffPost* published an article about COVID-19 protesters (Papenfuss 2020). White House adviser and member of a group calling themselves "Save Our Country" coalition, Stephen Moore, reportedly compared the individuals, who were in direct violation of Michigan's order, to civil rights icon, Rosa Parks. Moore stated they were "protesting against injustices and loss liberties." Moore reportedly told another news outlet that, "We need to be the Rosa Parks here, and protest against these government injustices." Moore is also a member of Trump's back-to-work council.

Mary Papenfuss (2020), the author of the *HuffPost* article, described the protests as part of a "new onslaught against Democratic-led states fueled by the Trump campaign." Nicole Hemmer, a historian, was quoted in the Papenfuss (2020) article. The Columbia University affiliated historian said the focus on "personal freedom" was actually an excuse for getting out and rallying against politicians they oppose. The lack of enforcement for violators of the protests have drawn comparisons to the military response to Black Lives Matters protests, which signals an immunity rooted in whiteness during the pandemic.

To further add fuel to the fire, Trump tweeted a message meant not only for the protestors but for his political base more broadly. He tweeted, "LIBERATE Michigan, Minnesota, and Virginia." In another tweet, he communicated more to his followers. On April 17, 2020, he tweeted, "LIBERATE Virginia and save your great 2nd Amendment. It is under siege." Additional protests were held following the tweets.

The protests in Michigan were organized by Michigan Conservative Coalition. The group is also known as Michigan Trump Republicans. The Michigan Freedom Fund, according to Papenfuss's (2020) article, promoted the protests. The group's official website states the group "fights to champion conservative policies on behalf of Michigan taxpayers." On the group's website it also states a commitment "to the principles of limited government, transparency in government, and the freedoms found in the Constitution. The Michigan Freedom Fund vows to 'protect Freedom.'"

In addition to the protests in Michigan, there were other ways that largely white people resisted or pushed back against local, state, and national orders. Many white evangelicals continued to hold in-person services. In Louisiana, a COVID-19 hot spot, the Life Tabernacle Church defied the state and national stay-at-home order. The pastor, Tony Spell, held Easter Sunday services on April 12, 2020. About 1,300 people attended the service, according to *Daily Mail*. The lawyer representing the pastor, Jeff Wittenbrink, eventually tested positive for COVID-19 and required hospitalization. Congregants in Kentucky and Florida also refused to comply with state and national measures to flatten the curve, resulting in the arrest of at least one pastor (Mazzei 2020). Additionally, Liberty University in Lynchburgh, Virginia, welcomed faculty, staff, and students back to campus as many colleges and universities transitioned to online instruction. By April 17, 2020, two employees and one student tested positive for COVID-19, reported Richmond.com.

While as many as eleven states included some form of exemptions for religious organizations, far too few complied with social distancing recommended guidelines. *ABC News* described the issue as a constitutional issue. "Religious institutions are widely believed to be protected from such regulations by the concept of church and state protected in the First Amendment. But whether that is actually the case is unclear." In the past, the Supreme Court has held "that a law cannot 'unduly burden' a specific religion unless there is a 'compelling interest' in doing so, and that burden must be applied equally to secular institutions." Liz Alesse, author of the *ABC News* article, "With constitutional questions murky, some churches continue to defy restrictions on gathers," also reported that the burden may be more of an issue for some religious groups than others. Some Jewish and Amish groups are not able to stream services online due to restrictions related to the use of electricity. Moreover, some religious groups, such as certain sects of Judaism require at least ten people in order to practice their religion. Aleese described this as a constitutional issue, "a tug-of-war . . . between some state and local governments over whether religious gatherings should be allowed while the coronavirus outbreak rages on."

Media accounts of the protests against stay-at-home orders and public discourse are missing very important points that American civil religion can explain. The key issues here are not chiefly about constitutional rights but a perceived threat against whiteness. Consequently, many members of the dominant group are rallying around the president's call for LIBERATION in defiance of his own administration's directives. The president is showing, as he has done in the past, a keen ability to tap into the fears of many people who fear that their perceived superior position at home and abroad is under attack. The fears run counter to the promises embedded in American civil religion. The fervent response to such perceived attacks on whiteness is best understood as religious. Whiteness is religious. Whiteness demands consolidation across various social and demographic groups (Martin 2021, 29–35).

Similarly, the attacks on the U.S. Capitol on January 6, 2021, can be understood as one of the greatest examples of how differently white and black people are treated in this country. Hundreds of mostly white people headed to Washington, D.C., in the hopes of protesting or stopping the peaceful transition of power from one administration to that next that is supposed to be a prized feature of American democracy. Instead, what happened was an insurrection at the U.S. Capitol that led to the deaths of more than one U.S. Capitol police officer. A total of five people died at the Capitol on that day, according to NPR. It was an event that terrorized and terrified the elected officials and their staffers who had no idea if they would live to see another day. White men and women stormed the Capitol and memorialized their actions live on social media or in photos. Some brazenly took images of government documents with their phones. Some participants were seen marching through the Capitol with Confederate flags and other hate symbols.

NPR published an article on July 2, 2021, chronicling "The Capitol Siege." The staff members described the arrests and some their stories. The publication described the event as a "riot" and said that it "has led to one of the largest criminal investigations in American history." The Federal Bureau of Investigation (FBI) considered the insurrection as a form of domestic terrorism. As of early July, over 530 people have been arrested for crimes related to the riot at the U.S. Capitol. NPR noted that "the defendants are predominately white and male. . . . Far-right militia members decked out in tactical gear allegedly rioted next to a county commissioner, a New York City sanitation work, and a two-time Olympic gold medalist." NPR (2021) also found that many of the people arrested had ties to extremist groups. For example, about thirty defendants showed support for QAnon, "the pro-Trump conspiracy theory."

Additionally, NPR (2021) found that more than thirty defendants were connected to the far-right group, the Proud Boys. "Their values have been widely described as racist, misogynist, anti-immigrant and hateful against minority groups."

Without question, if those were a group of majority black people storming the Capitol we would likely be having conversations now about a great massacre. More than six months removed from the horrifying events of that day, there are still debates happening in Congress and throughout the country about whether the U.S. government should even investigate what took place. As of July 1, 2021, House Speaker Nancy Pelosi selected individuals to serve on the select House committee that will look into the events on January 6, 2021, at the U.S. Capitol (CNBC 2001). Republican, Liz Cheney, was among the eight members selected. Representative Cheney was one of only two Republicans to support the creation of the committee. Cheney was also one of ten Republicans who favored impeaching President Trump for encouraging the assault on the Capitol as Congress counted the results from the November 2020 election. The election led to the ascension of former Vice President Joe Biden to the U.S. presidency. CNBC (2021) noted, "Underscoring the Republican resistance to starting another probe, McCarthy threatened to revoke GOP representatives' committee seats if they accepted an appointment to the panel from Pelosi."

It is clear that black and white people in America continue to experience life differently. Black people are expected to keep hope alive at the same time that the likelihood that the racial subordination of black people will change is hopeless. This is not the message that many black people want to hear but it is the reality of their experience in America. Racial realism provides the best framework for finding peace, agency, and power in the permanent racial subordination of black people as we continue to call out failures to recognize the dignity and humanity of black men, women, and children.

## NOTE

1. Parts of this chapter were previously published in *America in Denial* (2021), Albany, NY: SUNY Press and are used with permission.

# References

"A Clever Hero: Slave Revolt Leader Charles Deslondes." Tell Me More. NPR. February 2011.

"Affirmative Action History." University of Rhode Island. Retrieved from https://web.uri.edu/affirmativeaction/affirmative-action-history/. Accessed on July 4, 2021.

Abrams, Willie. 1992. "A Reply to Derrick Bell's Racial Realism." *Connecticut Law Review* 24, 2: 517–526.

Alba, Richard and Victor Nee. 2003. *Remaking the American Mainstream: Assimilation and Contemporary Immigration*, 1–66. Cambridge: Harvard University Press.

Alkon, Alison Hope, Sarah Bowen, Yuki Kato, Kara Alexis Young. 2020. "Unequally Vulnerable: A Food Justice Approach to Racial Disparities in COVID-19 Cases." *Agriculture and Human Values* 37, no. 1–2: 535–536.

Alozie, Nicolas. 1995. "Political Tolerance Hypotheses and White Opposition to a Martin Luther King Holiday in Arizona." *The Social Science Journal* 32, no. 1: 1–16.

"Antebellum Louisiana II." Retrieved from http://www.crt.state.la.us/louisiana-state-museum/online-exhibits/the-cabildo/antebellum-louisiana-agrarian-life/. Accessed on May 23, 2021.

Arias Elizabeth Arias, Norman J. Johnson, Tejada Betzaida Vera. 2020. "Racial Disparities in Mortality in the Adult Hispanic Population." *SSM—Population Health* 11: 1–10.

Bailey, Beth and David Farber. 2001. "The 'Double-V' Campaign in World War II Hawaii: African Americans, Racial Ideology, and Federal Power." *Journal of Social History* 26, no. 4: 817–843.

Baldwin, James. "American Dream and the American Negro." 1965. *New York Times*. https://www.nytimes.com/images/blogs/papercuts/baldwin-and-buckley.pdf

Banks, Patricia A. 2019. "High Culture, Black Culture: Strategic Assimilation and Cultural Steering in Museum Philanthropy." *Journal of Consumer Culture*, (May).

Bartscher, Alina, Mortiz Kuhn, Mortiz Schularick, and Paul Wachtel. 2021. "Monetary Policy and Racial Inequality." *Federal Reserve Bank of New York Staff Reports*, no. 959. https://www.newyorkfed.org/medialibrary/media/research/staff_reports/sr959.pdf.

Bell, Derrick. 1992. "Racial Realism." *Connecticut Law Review* 24, no. 2: 363–379.

Bell, Derrick. 1980. *Brown v. Board of Education* and the Interest-Convergence Dilemma. *Harvard Law Review*, 518–533.

Bellah, Robert. 1967. "Religion in America." *Dædalus, Journal of the American Academy of Arts and Sciences* 96, no. 1: 1–21.

Berry, Mary Frances. 1996. "Vindicating Martin Luther King, Jr.: The Road to a Color-Blind Society." *The Journal of Negro History* 81, no. 1/4: 137–144.

"The Best and Worst Cities for Black Women: 2021 Edition." Travel Noire. February 1, 2021. https://travelnoire.com/best-and-worst-us-cities-for-black-women-2021.

Bhutta, Neil, Andrew C. Chang, Lisa J. Dettling, and Joanne W. Hsu. 2020. "Disparities in Wealth by Race and Ethnicity in the 2019 Survey of Consumer Finances," FEDS Notes. Washington: Board of Governors of the Federal Reserve System, September 28, 2020, https://doi.org/10.17016/2380-7172.2797.

"Black Women and the Wealth Gap: Best Cities to Flourish Financially." January 30, 2021. https://www.moneygeek.com/living/best-cities-black-women/.

Boen, Courtney, Lisa Keister, and Brian Aronson. 2020. "Beyond Net Worth: Racial Differences in Wealth Portfolios and Black-White Health Inequality across the Life Course." *Journal of Health and Social Behavior* 61, no. 2: 153–169.

Bonilla-Silva, Eduardo and Gianpaolo Baiocchi. 2001. "Anything but Racism: How Sociologists Limit the Significance of Racism." *Race and Society* 4, no. 2: 117–31.

Bonilla-Silva, Eduardo. 1996. "Rethinking Racism: Toward a Structural Interpretation." *American Sociological Review* 62: 465–80.

Bonilla-Silva, Eduardo. 1999. "The Essential Social Fact of Race." *American Sociological Review* 64: 899–906.

Bonilla-Silva, Eduardo. 2001. *White Supremacy and Racism in the Post-Civil Rights Era. Boulder, CO:* Lynne Rienner Publishers.

Bonilla-Silva, Eduardo. 2002. "The Linguistics of Color Blind Racism: How to Talk Nasty about Blacks without Sounding 'Racist.'" *Critical Sociology* 28, no. 1–2: 41–64.

Bonilla-Silva, Eduardo. 2003. "'New Racism,' Color-Blind Racism, and the Future of Whiteness in America." In Ashley W. Doane and Eduardo Bonilla-Silva (eds.) *White Out: The Continuing Significance of Racism*. New York: Routledge.

Bonilla-Silva, Eduardo. 2012. "The Invisible Weight of Whiteness: The Racial Grammar of Everyday Life in Contemporary America." *Ethnic and Racial Studies* 35, no. 2: 173–94.

Bonilla-Silva, Eduardo. 2018. *Racism without Racists: Color-Blind Racism and the Persistence of Racial Inequality in America*. Lanham, MD: Rowman & Littlefield.

Bortolini, Mattaeo. 2021. "The Trap of Intellectual Success: Robert N. Bellah, the American Civil Religion Debate, and the Sociology of Knowledge." *Theory and Society* 41, no. 2: 187–210.

Bostdorff, Denise M. 2003. "George Bush's Post-September 11 Rhetoric of Covenant Renewal: Upholding the Faith of the Greatest Generation." *Quarterly Journal of Speech* 89, no. 4: 293–319.

Bradbury, Steven, Jim Lusted, and Jacco van Sterkenburg. 2021. *"Race," Ethnicity and Racism in Sports Coaching.* England, UK: Routledge.

Brooks, Jennifer E. 2000. "Winning the Peace: Georgia Veterans and the Struggle to Define the Political Legacy of World War II." *Journal of Southern History* 66, no. 3: 563–604.

Brown, Michael, Martin Carnoy, Elliot Currie, Troy Duster, David Oppenheimer, Marjorie Shultz, and David Wellman. 2003. *Whitewashing Race: The Myth of a Color-Blind Society.* Berkeley: University of California Press.

Buozis, Michael. 2018. "Bizarre Dissonances in Baltimore": Class and and Race in the Color-blind Discourses of Police Violence." *Democratic Communique* 27, no. 2: 36–52.

Burkett, Randall. 1978. *Garveyism as a Religious Movement: The Institutionalization of a Black Civil Religion.* New York: Oxford University Press.

Burnetts, Charles. 2016. "Of Basterds and the Greatest Generation: The Limits of Sentimentalism and the Post-Classical War Film." *Journal of Film and Video* 68, no. 2: 3–13.

Cahill, Peter A. 2021. "Sentencing Order and Memorandum Opinion." District Court. State of Minnesota. NPR. Retrieved from https://www.npr.org/sections/trial-over-killing-of-george-floyd/2021/06/25/1010385046/read-the-derek-chauvin-sentencing-decision. Accessed on July 4, 2021.

Carson, Clayborne. ed. 1998. *The Autobiography of Martin Luther King, Jr.* New York: Warner.

Carson, Tom. 2016. "Fables of Our Fathers." Retrieved from https://thebaffler.com/salvos/fables-of-our-fathers-carson. 161–169. Accessed May 25, 2021.

Carter, J. Scott, Cameron Lippard, and Andrew Baird. 2019. "Veiled Threats: Color-Blind Frames and Group Threat in Affirmative Action Discourse" *Social Problems* 66, 4: 503–518.

Chavez, Ernest. 2021. "Intrusions of Violence: Afro-Pessimism and Reading Social Death beyond Solitary Confinement." *Theoretical Criminology* 25, no. 1: 3–22.

Chow, Rosalind and Eric Knowles. 2015. "Taking Race Off the Table: Agenda Setting and Support for Color-Blind Public Policy." *Personality and Social Psychology Bulletin*, 1–15.

Clark, Alexis. 2020. "Black Americans Who Served in WWII Faced Segregation Abroad and at Home." *History.com.* Retrieved from https://www.history.com/news/black-soldiers-world-war-ii-discrimination. Accessed May 25, 2021.

Clark, Alexis. 2020. "Returning From War, Returning to Racism." *New York Times Magazine.* Retrieved from https://www.nytimes.com/2020/07/30/magazine/black-soldiers-wwii-racism.html. Accessed May 25, 2021.

Coates, Ta-Nehisi. 2014. "The Case for Reparations." *The Atlantic.* https://www.theatlantic.com/magazine/archive/2014/06/the-case-for-reparations/361631/.

Cohen, Geoffrey, Julio Garcia, Nancy Apfel, and Allison Master. 2006. "Reducing the Racial Achievement Gap: A Social-Psychological Intervention." *Science* 313: 1307–1310.

Collins, Chuck, Darrick Hamilton, Dedrick Asante-Muhammad, and Josh Hoxie. 2019. "Ten Solutions to Bridge the Racial Wealth Divide." The Ohio State University Krwan Institute for the Study of Race and Ethnicity, Institute for Policy Studies, NCRC, and Inequality.org.

Compton, John, W. 2019. "Why the Covenant Worked: On the Institutional Foundations of the American Civil Religion," *Religion* 10, no. 6: 350–367.

Copeland, Roy W. 2013. "In the Beginning: Origins of African American Real Property Ownership in the United States." *Journal of Black Studies* 44, no. 6: 646–664.

Couvillion, Ellyn. 2015. "Ashland-Belle Helene in Ascension Parish Restored to Former Glory; Historic Plantation Home Owned by Shell Chemical." *Advocate.* (Baton Rouge, LA), June 17.

"COVID-19 Racial and Ethnic Health Disparities." December 10, 2020. CDC. https://www.cdc.gov/coronavirus/2019-ncov/community/health-equity/racial-ethnic-disparities/index.html

Crockett, Walter Hobson. 2012–2013. "Becoming the 'Greatest Generation': Company B, 137th Infantry Regiment." *Kansas History* 35: 234–249.

Delgado, Richard and Jean Stefancic. 2001. *Critical Race Theory: An Introduction.* New York: New York University Press.

Dixon, LaTanya. 2020. "From Statehood to School Desegregation: Racial Disparities in the Public Education of Mississippi, 1817–1969." *AERA Open* 6, no. 4: 1–15.

Douglas, Frederick. 1851. "The Meaning of the Fourth of July to the Negro." https://www.pbs.org/wgbh/aia/part4/4h2927t.html

Du Bois, W. E. B. 1934. "A Negro Within a Nation." https://www.blackpast.org/african-american-history/1934-w-e-b-du-bois-negro-nation-within-nation/.

Du Bois, W. E. B. (William Edward Burghardt), 1868–1963. A pragmatic program for a dark minority, ca. 1935. W. E. B. Du Bois Papers (MS 312). Special Collections and University Archives, University of Massachusetts Amherst Libraries

Du Bois, W. E. B. (William Edward Burghardt), 1868–1963. A sermon for the churchman, ca. 1948. W. E. B. Du Bois Papers (MS 312). Special Collections and University Archives, University of Massachusetts Amherst Libraries.

Du Bois, W. E. B. (William Edward Burghardt), 1868–1963. American Negroes, socialism and communism, May 21, 1958. W. E. B. Du Bois Papers (MS 312). Special Collections and University Archives, University of Massachusetts Amherst Libraries.

Du Bois, W. E. B. (William Edward Burghardt), 1868–1963. Negro property, August 1910. W. E. B. Du Bois Papers (MS 312). Special Collections and University Archives, University of Massachusetts Amherst Libraries.

Du Bois, W. E. B. (William Edward Burghardt), 1868–1963. On the future of the American Negro, March 1953. W. E. B. Du Bois Papers (MS 312). Special Collections and University Archives, University of Massachusetts Amherst Libraries.

Du Bois, W. E. B. (William Edward Burghardt), 1868–1963. The winds of time, June 12, 1948. W. E. B. Du Bois Papers (MS 312). Special Collections and University Archives, University of Massachusetts Amherst Libraries.

Du Bois, W. E. B. [1899] 2014. *The Philadelphia Negro: A Social Study.* New York: Oxford University Press.

Du Bois, W. E. B. 1998. *Black Reconstruction.* New York: Free Press.

## References

Du Bois, W. E. B. 1897. "Conservation of the Races." https://teachingamericanhistory.org/library/document/the-conservation-of-races/.

Du Bois, W. E. B. [1903] 1993. *The Souls of Black Folk*. Reprint, New York: Knopf.

Dye, K. 2020. "The Debate on Reparations before the Debate on Reparations at the National Bank Economic Development Conference in Detroit, 1969." *Michigan Historical Review* 46, no. 2: 175–186.

Elfenbein, Andrew. 2020. "Statement Regarding the Death of George Floyd." University of Minnesota. https://cla.umn.edu/english/news-events/news/statement-regarding-death-george-floyd. Accessed on July 4, 2021.

Ekovich, Steven R. 2017. "Listening to Donald Trump." *Contemporary French & Francophone Studies* 21, no. 5: 498–506.

Fanon, Frantz. 1952, 2008. *Black Skin, White Masks*. Translated by Richard Philcox. New York: Grove Press.

Fasching-Varner, Kenneth, Roland Mitchell, Lori Latrice Martin, and Karen Benton-Haron. 2014. Beyond School-to-Prison Pipeline and toward an Educational and Penal Realism. *Equity & Excellence in Education* 47, no. 4: 410–429.

Feagin, Joe and Melvin Sikes. 1994. *Living with Racism: The Black Middle Class Experience*. Boston, MA: Beacon Press.

Feagin, Joe R. 2004. "Toward an Integrated Theory of Systemic Racism." In Maria Krysan and Amanda E. Lewis (eds) *The Changing Terrain of Race and Ethnicity*, 203–223. New York: Russell Sage Foundation.

Feagin, Joe and Sean Elias. 2013. "Rethinking Racial Formation Theory: A Systemic Racism Critique." *Ethnic and Racial Studies* 36, no. 6: 931–960.

Feagin, Joe. 1991. "The Continuing Significance of Race: Antiblack Discrimination in Public Places." *American Sociological Review* 56: 101–16.

Feagin, Joe. 2013. *Systemic Racism: A Theory of Oppression*: New York, Routledge.

Feagin. Joe. 2006. "Chapter One." *Systemic Racism: A Theory of Oppression*. New York: Routledge.

Fessenden, Marissa. "How a Nearly Successful Slave Revolt Was Intentionally Lost to History." *Smithsonian Magazine*. Retrieved from http://www.smithsonianmag.com/smart-news/its-anniversary-1811-louisiana-slave-revolt-180957760/. Accessed by June 12, 2017.

Finley, Stephen C., Gray, Biko, and Martin, Lori Latrice Martin. 2018. "Affirming Our Values: African American Scholars, White Virtual Mobs, and the Complicity of White University Administrators." *Journal of Academic Freedom* 9: 1–20.

Finley, Stephen C., Biko Gray, and Lori Latrice Martin. 2020. *The Religion of White Rage: White Workers, Religious Fervor, and the Myth of Black Racial Progress*. Edinburg University Press.

Finley, Stephen C. 2012. "The Meaning of *Mother* in Louis Farrakhan's 'Mother Wheel': Race, Gender, Sexuality in the Cosmology of the Nation of Islam's UFO." *Journal of the American Academy of Religion* 80, no. 2: 434–465.

Finley, Stephen C. 2013. "Hidden Away: Esotericism and Gnosticism in Elijah Muhammad's Nation of Islam." In *Histories of the Hidden God: Concealment and Revelation in Western Gnostic, Esoteric, and Mystical Traditions*. Edited by April DeConick and Grant Adamson. London: Acumen Publishing, 259–80.

Follett, Richard. *The Sugar Masters: Planters and Slaves in Louisiana Cane World, 1820-1860.* Baton Rouge: Louisiana Press.

Fong, Kelvin, Maayan Yitshak-Sade, Kevin Lane, Patricia M. Fabian, Itai Kloog, Joel Schwartz, Brent Coull, Petros Koutrakis, Jaime Hart, Francine Laden, and Antonella Zanobetti. 2020. "Racial Disparities in Associations between Neighborhood Demographic Polarization and Birth Weight." *International Journal of Environmental Research and Public Health* 17, no. 9: 3076–3085.

Fontana, David. 2010. "Obama and the American Civil Religion from the Political Left." *George Washington International Law Review* 41, no. 4: 909–912.

Frazier, E. Franklin. 1939. *The Negro Family in the United States.* Chicago: University of Chicago Press.

Frazier, E. Franklin. 1949. "Race Contacts and the Social Structure." *American Sociological Review* 14, no. 1: 1–11.

Frazier, E. Franklin. 1957. *Black Bourgeoisie.* Glencoe: Free Press.

Frazier, E. Franklin. 1927. "The Pathology of Racial Prejudice." *The Forum* 70: 856–862.

Frey, Sophie. 2016. "Black and White Veterans and the GI Bill." Dartmouth. History 90.01: Topics in Digital History. Retrieved from https://journeys.dartmouth.edu/censushistory/2016/10/31/black-and-white-veterans-and-the-gi-bill/. Accessed on May 25, 2021.

Gedicks, Frederick. 2010. "American Civil Religion: An Idea Whose Time Is Past." *George Washington International Law Review* 41 no. 4: 891–908.

Glenn, Evelyn Nakano. 1992. "From Servitude to Service Work: Historical Continuities in the Racial Division of Paid Reproductive Labor." *Signs* 18, no. 1: 1–43

Goldberg, Simon, John Fortney, Jessica Chen, Bessie Young, Karen Lehavot, and Tracy Simpson. 2020. "Military Service and Military Health Care Coverage are Associated with Reduced Racial Disparities in Time to Mental Health Treatment Initiation." *Administrative Policy Mental Health* 47, no. 4: 555–568.

Goodman, Laurie and Christopher Mayer. 2018. "Homeownership and the American Dream." *Journal of Economic Perspectives* 32, no. 1: 31–58.

Gray, Biko, Stephen C. Finley, and Lori Latrice Martin. 2019. "High-Tech Lynching: White Virtual Mobs and University Administrators as Policing Agents in Higher Education." *Issues in Race and Society.* 8:147–176.

Hammond, Philip E. 1994. "Forum: American Civil Religion Revisited." *Religion & American Culture* 4, no. 1:1–7.

Harper, Shaun R. 2018. "Black Male Student-Athletes and Racial Inequities in NCAA Division I College Sports." USC Race and Equity Center. https://race.usc.edu/wp-content/uploads/2020/08/Pub-2-Harper-Sports-Reports.pdf.

Harris, Cheryl. 1993. "Whiteness as Property," *Harvard Law Review*, 106, no. 8: 1707–1791.

Harris, Frederick. 1999. *Something Within: Religion in African American Activism.* New York: Oxford University Press.

Hartman, Saidiya and Frank B. Wilderson, III. 2003. "The Unthought." *Qui Parle* 13, no. 2 (Spring).

Hartman, Saidiya. *Scenes of Subjection: Terror, Slavery and Self-Making in Nineteenth-Century America.* New York: Oxford University Press, 1997.
Headly, Andrea and James E. Wright. 2020. "Is Representation Enough? Racial Disparities in Levels of Force and Arrests by Policy." *Public Administration Review* 80, no. 6: 1051–1062.
Higginbotham, Evelyn. 1993. *Righteous Discontent.* Cambridge: Harvard University Press.
Higginbotham, Evelyn. 1992. "African American Women's History and the Metalanguage of Race." *Signs* 17, 2: 251–274.
Hiller, Amy E. 2003. "Redlining the Home Owners' Loan Corporation." *Journal of Urban History* 29, no. 4: 394–420.
Hine, Darlene Clark, Stanley Harrold, and Willie Hine. *African American Odyssey.* Boston: Pearson, 2010.
Hinson, Waymon. 2018. "Land Gains, Land Losses: The Odyssey of African Americans Since Reconstruction." *American Journal of Economics & Sociology* 77, no. 3/4: 893–939.
HoSang, Daniel, Oneka LaBennett, and Laura Pulido, eds. 2012. *Racial Formation in the Twenty-First Century.* Berkeley: University of California Press (ebook).
Hucks, Tracey. 2012. *Yoruba Traditions and African American Religious Nationalism.* Albuquerque: University of New Mexico Press.
Jackson, Kenneth. 1980. "Race, Ethnicity, and Real Estate Appraisal: The Home Owners Loan Corporation and the Federal Housing Administration." *Journal of Urban History* 6, no. 4: 419–452.
Jefferson, Robert F. 2003. "Enabled Courage": Race, Disability, and Black World War II Veterans in Postwar America." *The Historian.* 65, no. 5: 1102–1124.
Jimenez, Tomás and Adam L. Horowitz. 2013. "When White Is Just Alright: How Immigrants Redefine Achievement and Reconfigure the Ethnoracial Hierarchy." *American Sociological Review* 78, no. 5: 849–871.
Jung, Moon Kie. 2009. "The Racial Unconscious of Assimilation Theory." *Du Bois Review.*
Jung, Moon-Kie and Yaejoon Kwon. 2013. "Theorizing the US Racial State: Sociology Since Racial Formation." *Sociology Compass* 7, no. 11: 927–940.
Jung, Mun-kie. 2015. *Beneath the Surface of White Supremacy: Denaturalizing U.S. Racisms Past and Present.* Stanford, CA: Stanford University Press.
Kahrl, Andrew. 2019. "Black People's Land Was Stolen." *New York Times.* June 20, 2019.
Kang, Kelly. 2021. "Survey of Earned Doctorates." National Science Foundation. National Center for Science and Engineering Statistics. https://ncses.nsf.gov/pubs/nsf21308/data-tables.
Katznelson, Ira and Suzanne Mettler. 2008. "On Race and Policy History: A Dialogue about the G.I. Bill." *Perspectives on Politics* 6, no. 3: 519–537.
Kauflin, Jeff and Janet Novack. 2021. "5 Big Ideas to Narrow the Racial Wealth Gap." *Forbes.* https://www.forbes.com/sites/jeffkauflin/2020/06/25/five-big-ideas-to-narrow-the-racial-wealth-gap/?sh=588b86a551ac.

King, Martin Luther. 1963. "Letter from the Birmingham Jail." https://www.africa.upenn.edu/Articles_Gen/Letter_Birmingham.html.

King, Martin Luther. 1964. "I Have a Dream." https://kingsinstitute.stanford.edu/king-papers/documents/i-have-dream-address-delivered-march-washington-jobs-and-freedom.

King, Martin Luther. 1967. *Where Do We Go from Here?* Boston, MA: Beacon Press.

Kollmann, Trevor M. and Price V. Fishback. 2011. "The New Deal, Race, and Home Ownership in the 1920s and 1930s." *American Economic Review* 101, no. 3: 366–370.

Kramer, Margaret. 2019. "A Timeline of Key Supreme Court Cases on Affirmative Action." *New York Times*. Retrieved from https://www.nytimes.com/2019/03/30/us/affirmative-action-supreme-court.html. Accessed on July 4, 2021.

Kuo, Susan and Benjamin Means. 2021. "A Corporate Law Rationale for Reparations." *Boston College Law Review* 62, no. 3: 800–850.

Lacy, Karyn. 2007. *Blue Chip Black Chip.* Berkeley: University of California Press.

Latty, Yvonne and Ron Tarver. 2005. "We Were There: Voices of African American Veterans, from World War II to the War in Iraq." New York: Amistad.

Lawlor, Ruth. 2019. "Second World War's Legacy of Racism." YaleGlobal Online. https://yaleglobal.yale.edu/content/second-world-wars-legacy-racism. Accessed on May 25, 2021.

Le, David. 2020. "'Monuments of Folly': Frederick Douglass, Charlottesville, and the National Religions of America." *Journal of the American Academy of Religion* 88, no. 3: 749–778.

Leonardo, Zeus and Ezekiel Dixon-Roman. 2018. "Post-Colorblindness: Or, Racialized Speech after Symbolic Racism." *Educational Philosophy & Theory* 50, 14: 1386–1387.

Lieberman-Cribbin, Wil, Stephanie Tuminello, Raja Flores, and Emanuela Taioli. "Disparities in COVID-19 Testing and Positivity in New York City." *American Journal of Preventative Medicine* 59, no. 3: 326–332.

Lincoln, Quillian. 2006. "New Approaches to Understanding Racial Prejudice and Discrimination." *Annual Review of Sociology* 32: 299–328.

Mansky, Jackie. 2016. "The Origins of the Term 'Affirmative Action.'" Smithsonian Magazine. https://www.smithsonianmag.com/history/learn-origins-term-affirmative-action-180959531/. Accessed on July 4, 2021.

Martin, Lori Latrice. 2019. *Big Box Schools: Race, Education, and the Danger of the Wal-Martization of Public Schools in America.* Lanham, MD: Lexington Books.

Martin, Lori Latrice. 2010. "Strategic Assimilation or Creation of Symbolic Blackness: Middle-Class Blacks in Suburban Contexts." *Journal of African American Studies*, 14, no. 2: 234–246.

Martin, Lori Latrice. Forthcoming. "Race, Abdul-Rauf, and Religious Realism." In J. Sholes and R. Balmer (eds) *Religion and Sport in North America.* New York: Taylor & Francis/Routledge.

Martin, Lori Latrice and Kenneth Fasching-Varner. 2017. "Race, Residential Segregation and the Death of Democracy: Education and Myths of Post-Racialism." *Democracy and Education.* 25, no. 1: 1–10.

Martin, Lori Latrice. 2013. *Black Asset Poverty and the Enduring Racial Divide.* Boulder, CO: First Forum Press, a Division of Lynne Rienner Publishers.

Martin, Lori Latrice. 2015. *White Sports Black Sports.* Santa Barbara, CA: Praeger Publishers.

Martin, Lori Latrice. 2019. "Race, Wealth, and Homesteading Revisited: How Public Policies Destroy(ed) Black Wealth." In J. Grimm and J. Loke (eds) *How Public Policy Impacts Racial Inequality,* 140–165. Baton Rouge: LSU Press.

Martin, Lori Latrice. Forthcoming. *The Untold Story of Abe Hawkins.* Book manuscript.

Martinez, Judy Perry. 2020. "ABA President Judy Perry Martinez Statement Re: Events in Minneapolis, Elsewhere and Equal Justice." American Bar Association. Retrieved from https://www.americanbar.org/news/abanews/aba-news-archives/2020/05/aba-president-judy-perry-martinez-statement-re--events-in-minnea/. Accessed on July 4, 2021.

Massey, Douglass and Nancy Denton. 1993. *American Apartheid: Segregation and the Making of the Underclass.* Cambridge, MA: Harvard University Press.

Mathisen, James. 1989. "Twenty Years after Bellah: Whatever Happened to American Civil Religion?" *Sociological Analysis* 50, no. 2: 129–146.

Mentch, Lucas. 2020. "On Racial Disparities in Recent Fatal Police Shootings." *Statistics and Public Policy* 7, no. 1: 9–18.

McDonald, Jermaine. 2013. "A Fourth Time of Trial: Towards an Implicit and Inclusive American Civil Religion." *Implicit Religion* 16, no. 1: 47–64.

McKinzie, Lindsay. 2020. "Words Matter for College Presidents, but So Will Actions." Insider Higher Ed. Retrieved from https://www.insidehighered.com/news/2020/06/08/searching-meaningful-response-college-leaders-killing-george-floyd. Accessed on July 4, 2021.

Mehkeri, Zainab A. Mehkeri. 2014. "Predatory Lending: What's Race Got to Do with It." *Public Interest Law. Reporter.* 44, no. 1: 43–52. Available at: http://lawecommons.luc.edu/pilr/vol20/iss1/9.

Messer, Chris M., Thomas E. Shriver, and Alison E. Adams. 2018. "The Destruction of Black Wall Street: Tulsa's 1921 Riot and the Eradication of Accumulated Wealth." *American Journal of Economics & Sociology* 77, no. 3/4: 789–819.

"Military Service History and VA Benefit Utilization Statistics." 2017. Department of Veterans Affairs. National Center for Veterans Analysis and Statistics. Retrieved from https://www.va.gov/vetdata/docs/SpecialReports/Minority_Veterans_Report.pdf. Accessed on May 25, 2021.

Mills, Charles "White Supremacy as a Sociopolitical System: A Philosophical Perspective." In Ashley W. Doane and Eduardo Bonilla-Silva (eds) *White Out: The Continuing Significance of Racism,* 35–48. Montreal, Canada: McGill-Queen's University Press.

Mills, Charles. 1997. *The Racial Contract.* Ithaca: Cornell University Press.

"Minnesota State Bar Association, Hennepin County Bar Association, Ramsey County Bar Association, and Minnesota Chapter of the Federal Bar Association Statement on George Floyd." 2020. Minnesota State Bar Association. Retrieved from https://www.mnbar.org/ramsey-county-bar-association/news/announcements/2020/06/01/

minnesota-state-bar-association-hennepin-county-bar-association-ramsey-county-bar-association-and-minnesota-chapter-of-the-federal-bar-association-statement-on-george-floyd-rcba. Accessed on July 4, 2021.

"MoneyGeek Lists the Best and Worst Cities for Black Women to Flourish Financially." February 1, 2021. Black Enterprise. https://www.blackenterprise.com/moneygeek-lists-the-best-and-worst-cities-for-black-women-to-flourish-financially/.

Moots, Glenn. 2010. "The Protestant Roots of American Civil Religion." *Humanitas* XXIII, nos. 1 and 2: 78–106.

Morrison, Toni. 2019. "The Slavebody and the Blackbody." In *The Source of Self-Regard: Selected Essays, Speeches, and Meditations*, 74–78. New York: Knopf.

"Myth & Reality." University of Rhode Island. Retrieved from https://web.uri.edu/affirmativeaction/myth-reality/. Accessed on July 4, 2021.

Noguera, Pedro A. 2008. "Creating Schools Where Race Does Not Predict Achievement." *The Journal of Negro Education* 77, no. 2: 90–103.

NPR Staff. 2021. "The Capitol Siege: The Arrested and Their Stories."

Olaloku-Teriba, Annie. 2018. "Afro-Pessimism and the (Un)Logic of Anti-Blackness." *Historical Materialism* 26, no. 2: 96–122.

Oliver, Melvin and Thomas Shapiro. 1995. *Black Wealth White Wealth*. New York: Routledge.

Omi, Michael and Howard Winant. 1994. *Racial Formation in the United States: From the 1960s to the 1990s*. New York: Routledge.

Onkst, David H. 2001. "'First a Negro . . . Incidentally a Veteran': Black World War Two Veterans and the G.I. Bill of Rights in the Deep South, 1944–1948." *Journal of Social History* 31, no. 3: 517–543.

Owens, Jayanti and Sara S. McLanahan. 2020. "Unpacking the Drivers of Racial Disparities in School Suspension and Expulsion." *Social Forces* 98, no. 4: 1548–1577.

Park, Robert. 1914. "Racial Assimilation in Secondary Groups with Particular Reference to the Negro." *American Journal of Sociology* 19, no. 5: 606–623.

Parks, Gregory Scott. 2008. "Towards a Critical Race Realism." *Cornell Journal of Law and Public Policy* 17, no. 3: 1–65.

Patterson, Orlando. 1982. *Slavery and Social Death: A Comparative Study*. Cambridge: Harvard University Press.

Perea, Juan F. 2014. "Doctrines of Delusion: How the History of the G.I. Bill and Other Inconvenient Truths Undermine the Supreme Court's Affirmative Action Jurisprudence." *University of Pittsburgh Law Review* 75, no. 4: 583–651.

Perrin, Andrew. 2020. "23% of Users in U.S. Say Social Media Led Them to Change Views on an Issue; Some Cite Black Lives Matter." Pew Research Center. Retrieved from https://www.pewresearch.org/fact-tank/2020/10/15/23-of-users-in-us-say-social-media-led-them-to-change-views-on-issue-some-cite-black-lives-matter/. Accessed on July 4, 2021.

Pinn, Anthony. 2020. "What Can Be Said? African American Religious Thought, Afro-Pessimism, and the Question of Hope." *Black Theology: An International Journal* 18, no. 2: 144–157.

Portes, Alejandro and Min Zhou. 1993. "The New Second Generation: Segmented Assimilation and its Variants." *Annals of the American Academy of Political and Social Science* 530: 74–96

Pritchard, Anita, and Michael Wiatrowski. 2008. "Race and Capital Punishment: State Level Analysis of the Effects of Race on States' Capital Punishment Policies." *Journal of Ethnicity in Criminal Justice* 6, no. 2: 103–121.

Pramuk, Jacob. 2021. "Pelosi Names 8 Members of January 6 Committee, including Republican Liz Chaney, to Probe Pro-Trump Riot." CNBC.com.

Rabouin, Dion. 2021. "10 Myths about the Racial Wealth Gap." *Axios*. https://www.axios.com/racial-wealth-gap-ten-myths-d14fe524-fec6-41fc-9976-0be71bc23aec.html.

Ray, Rashawn. 2020. "Why Are Blacks Dying at Higher Rates from COVID-19?" Brookings, April 9. https://www.brookings.edu/blog/fixgov/2020/04/09/why-are-blacks-dying-at-higher-rates-from-covid-19/.

Rayasam, Renuka and Ben White. 2021. "Biden's Big Challenge: A Growing Racial Wealth Gap." *Politico.com*. https://www.politico.com/news/2020/11/18/racial-wealth-gap-biden-437177.

Sabella, Jeremy. 2019. "Postures of Piety and Protest: American Civil Religion and the Politics of Kneeling in the NFL." *Religions* 10, no. 8: 449–466.

Sakhuja, Swati, Mackenzie Fowler, and Akinyemi Ojesina. 2021. "Race/Ethnicity, Sex and Insurance Disparities in Colorectal Cancer Screening among Individuals with and without Cardiovascular Disease." *Preventative Medicine Reports* 21: 1–8.

Saperstein, Aliya, Andrew Penner, and Ryan Light. 2013. "Racial Formation in Perspective: Connecting Individuals, Institutions, and Power Relations." *Annual Review of Sociology* 39, no. 1: 359.

Saravia, Catarina. 2021. "Low US Rates Exacerbate Racial Wealth Gap, Paper Shows." https://www.bloomberg.com/news/articles/2021-01-29/low-u-s-rates-exacerbate-racial-wealth-gap-paper-shows.

Schaeffer, Katherine. 2020. "On 75th Anniversary of V-E Day, about 300,000 American WWII Veterans are Alive." Pew Research. https://www.pewresearch.org/fact-tank/2020/05/08/on-75th-anniversary-of-v-e-day-about-300000-american-wwii-veterans-are-alive/. Access on May 25, 2021.

Semega, Jessica, Melissa Kollar, and John F. Creamer. 2020. "Income and Poverty in the United States: 2019." U.S. Census Bureau. Washington, D.C. https://www.census.gov/content/dam/Census/library/publications/2020/demo/p60-270.pdf.

Sexton, Jared. 2011. "The Social Life of Social Death: On Afro-Pessimism and Black Optimism." *Tensions* 5, 1–47.

Shapiro, Thomas. 2001. *Assets for the Poor: The Benefits of Spreading Asset Ownership*. New York: Russell Sage Foundation.

Shapiro, Thomas, Tatjana Meschede, and Sam Osoro. 2013. "The Roots of the Widening Racial Wealth Gap: Explaining the Black-White Economic Divide." Institute on Assets and Social Policy, Brandeis University.

Sherman, William Tecumseh. January 16, 1865. "Special Field Order No. 15: Forty Acres and a Mule."

Shupe, Kevin. "John H. Rudolph Papers. Retried from http://www.lib.lsu.edu/sites/default/files/sc/findaid/0355.pdf. 2009. Accessed on May 23, 2021.

Silver, Adam. 2020. "Memo from NBA Commissioner Adam Silver to League Employees." National Basketball Association. Retrieved from https://www.nba.com/news/silver-statement-nba-employees. Accessed on July 4, 2021.

Sitarik, Alexandra, Suzanne Havstad, Haejin Kim, Edward Zoratti, Dennis Ownby, Christine Cole Johnson, and Ganesa Wegineka. "Racial Disparities in Allergic Outcomes Persist to Age 10 Years in Black and White Children." Annals of Allergy, Asthma & Immunology 124, no. 4: 342–349.

"Slavery in Louisiana." n.d. Retrieved from http://www.whitneyplantation.com/slavery-in-louisiana.html. Accessed on May 23, 2021.

Spader, Jonathan and Christopher Herbert. 2017. "Waiting for Homeownership: Assessing the Future of Homeownership, 2015–2035." *Boston College Environmental Affairs Law Review* 44, no. 2: 267–294.

Stefancic, Jean. 2018. "Law, Religion, and Racial Justice: A Comment on Derrick Bell's Last Article." *Case Western Reserve Law Review* 69, no. 2: 341–354.

"Study: Shreveport No. 134 for Black Women." February 2, 2021. *Shreveport Times*. https://www.shreveporttimes.com/story/news/2021/02/14/best-cities-black-women-owned-businesses-study/6708725002/.

Sullivan, Laura and Tatjana Meschede. 2018. "How Measurement of Inequalities in Wealth by Race/Ethnicity Impacts Narrative and Policy: Investigating the Full Distribution." *Race and Social Problems* 10, no. 1: 19–29.

Taylor, George. 2004. "Racism as 'The Nation's Crucial Sin': Theology and Derrick Bell." *Michigan Journal of Race and Law* 9: 1–55.

Taylor, Miles, S. Min, and K. Reid. 2020. "Cumulative Inequality at the End of Life?: Racial Disparities in Impairment in the Time Before Death." *The Journals of Gerontology: Series B* 75, no. 6: 1292–1301.

Teaching American History website. http://teachingamericanhistory.org/library/document/the-conservation-of-races/.

Telles, Edward and Vilma Ortiz. 2008. *Generations of Exclusion: Mexican Americans, Assimilation, and Race*. Russell Sage Foundation.

Thakore, Bhoomi K. 2014. "Maintaining the Mechanisms of Colorblind Racism in the Twenty-First Century." *Humanity & Society* 38, no. 1: 3.

Thomas, Deja and Juliana Menasce Horowitz. 2020. "Support for Black Lives Matter Has Decreased Since June but Remains Strong Among Black Americans." Pew Research Center. Retrieved from https://www.pewresearch.org/fact-tank/2020/09/16/support-for-black-lives-matter-has-decreased-since-june-but-remains-strong-among-black-americans/. Accessed on July 4, 2021.

Thomas, Melvin, Cedric Herring, Hayward Derrick Horton, Moshe Semyonov, Loren Henderson, and Patrick L. Mason. 2020. "Race and the Accumulation of Wealth: Racial Differences in Net Worth over the Life Course, 1989–2009." *Social Problems* 67, no. 1: 20–39.

Ture, Kwame and Charles Hamilton. 1992. *Black Power: The Politics of Liberation.* New York: Vintage Books.

Turner, Sarah and John Bound. 2002. "Closing the Gap or Widening the Divide: The Effects of the G.I. Bill and World War II on the Educational Outcomes of Black Americans." *The Journal of Economic History* 63, no. 1: 145–177.

Valdes, Francisco. 2014. "Critical Race Action: Queer Lessons and Seven Legacies from the One and Only Derrick Bell." University of Miami School of Law Institutional Repository, 1–23.

Wang, Qiang, Mei-Po Kwan, Jie Fan, and Jian Lin. 2021. "Racial Disparities in Energy Poverty in the United States." *Renewable & Sustainable Energy Review* 137: 1–12.

Weiss, Jana. 2017. "Remember, Celebrate, and Forget? The Martin Luther King Day and the Pitfalls of Civil Religion." *Journal of American Studies* 53, no. 2: 428–448.

Whillcock, Rita Kirk. 1994. "Dream Believers: The Unifying Visions and Competing Values of Adherents to American Civil Religion. *Presidential Studies Quarterly* 24, no. 2: 375–388.

White, Rebecca. "Left Out of the 'Greatest Generation.'" *The Wilson Quarterly* 39, no. 1: 1–6.

White, Valerie. 2021. "How We Close the Racial Wealth Gap." *New York Times.* April 15, 2021. https://www.amny.com/coronavirus/op-ed-how-we-close-the-racial-wealth-gap/.

Wilderson III, Frank B. 2010. *Red, White, and Black.* Durham, NC: Duke University Press.

William, Julius Wilson. 1978. *The Declining Significance of Race.* Chicago: University of Chicago Press.

Williams, Chad L. 2007. "Vanguards of the New Negro: African American Veterans and Post-World War I Racial Militancy." *The Journal of African American History* 92, no. 3: 347–370.

Yancy, George. 2018. *Backlash: What Happens When We Can Talk Honestly about Racism in America.* Lanham, MD: Rowman & Littlefield.

Yi, Jacqueline and Nathan R. Todd. 2021. "Internalized Model Minority Myth Among Asian Americans: Links to Anti-Black Attitudes and Opposition to Affirmative Action." Cultural Diversity and Ethnic Minority Psychology. Advance online publication. https://doi.org/10.1037/cdp0000448. Accessed on July 4, 2021.

Zelner, Jon, Rob Trangucci, Ramya Naraharisetti, Alex Cao, Ryan Malosh, Kelly Broen, Nina Masters, Paul Delamater. "Racial Disparities in Coronavirus Disease 2019 (COVID-19) Mortality Are Driven by Unequal Infection Risks." *Clinical Infectious Diseases*, https://doi.org/10.1093/cid/ciaa1723.

# Index

104th U.S. Colored Troops, 68
1935 National Labor Relations Act, 107
24th Infantry Regiment, 70, 73
369th Regiment Harlem, 69, 71
54th Massachusetts Colored Infantry Regiment, 68

Abdul-Rauf, Mamoud, 37–39, 42
abuse, 80, 112
academic outcomes, 2
achievement gap, 2
activism, 18–19, 84, 110
*Adarand Constructors, Inc. v. Pena,* 105
Administrators, 56, 77, 94, 109–10
admissions policy, 5
affirmative action, 26, 32, 56, 88, 101, 103–15
African American religion, 21, 89
African American Studies, 1, 22
African Liberation Movement, 63
Afro-Pessimism, 22, 30–31
aggravating factors, 112–13
Alexander, Fred, 81
Ali, Muhammad, 39
All Lives Matter, 110
American Civil Religion, 12–15, 36–39, 42, 83–93, 118–19, 122
American dream, 16, 18, 26
American Expeditionary Force, 69

American individualism, 88
American national religion, 15
American Negro Academy, 23
American Revolution, 5, 36, 67, 86
anti-black, 1, 11–12, 19–20, 24, 27, 30–36, 42, 67, 73, 79, 82, 96, 106–10
anti-intellectualism, 2
assault, 12, 53, 70, 80–81, 85, 113, 123
asset inequality, 43, 45
asset poverty, 19, 43, 45, 47, 39, 93
assets, 19, 49, 45, 47, 49, 93
assimilation, 1–2, 17, 27, 35, 41, 96, 119
authority, 13, 75, 87, 112
avoidance, 26, 86

baby bonds, 63
backlash, 10, 38–39, 56, 90–101, 103
*Bakke v. University of California Board of Regents (1978),* 11, 32, 105–7
Baldwin, James, 16, 18
Baltimore, Maryland, 118
banks, 49, 59, 62, 64, 75–76
barriers, 3–4, 40, 55, 68, 75, 88, 116, 118
Baton Rouge Bus Boycott, 10
Baton Rouge, Louisiana, 10, 72
beliefs, 13–14, 32, 74, 84–85, 89

Bell, Derrick, 19–46, 65, 82–83, 88, 101, 103, 114–15
benchmarks, 107
Biden, Joe, 64
biological arguments, 2
biology, 24, 100
black asset poverty, 43, 45, 47, 93
black athletes, 36
black deaths, 114
Black Lives Matter, 20, 39, 84, 101, 103–16
Black National Economic Conference, 62
black power, 19, 83–102
black professors, 94
black veterans, 76, 78, 80
Black Wall Street, 58
black-owned businesses, 105
blackness, 11, 31, 38–39, 85, 89, 95, 107
boycotts, 10, 71–77, 84, 87
Brooks Park, 9
*Brown v. Board of Education of Topeka, Kansas (1954)*, 10, 12, 31, 84, 86
Brown, Michael, 108
Bullard, Eugene, 69–70
Bush, George, 78–79

Cahill, Peter, 111–14
cancer screening, 5
capitalism, 62
cardiovascular disease, 5
Carlos, John, 39, 109
Carney, Williams, 68
caste, 16, 25, 79
caste school, 25
Central Park Five, 12
charges, 29, 71
Chauvin, Dereck, 111–114
Christian, 17–18, 36–37, 62, 76, 88–91, 119
Christian masculinity, 119
*City of Richmond v. Croson*, 105
civic engagement, 109

civil rights, 10, 25–26, 33–34, 38, 54, 56, 72–73, 79–80, 82–106
Civil Rights Act of 1964, 10, 106
civil rights movement, 7, 10, 14, 19, 36, 73, 78, 104
Civil War, 7–10, 13, 36, 50, 68–69, 80, 86
civilian population, 4
civilization, 17, 23
Clinton, Bill, 21, 23, 105
Clinton, Hillary, 12
coaches, 5–6, 40–41, 120
collective action, 109
collective life, 24
college, 3, 5–7, 20, 23, 46, 49, 64, 76, 101, 105–06, 108–11, 114, 120, 122
college sports, 5–6
colonialism, 22, 28, 96
colorblind, 15, 19, 88–90, 101
colorblind racism, 19, 22
colorblind rhetoric, 15
Committee on Equal Employment Opportunity, 103
Constitution, 13, 36–37, 99, 104–05, 121–22
convergence, 26, 30–31, 34
conviction, 111
coping strategies, 26
counseling, 2
counternarratives, 98
covenants, 31, 78
COVID-19, 3–4, 20, 37, 86, 100, 117–24
crack epidemic, 119
criminal history, 112
criminal justice system, 22
criminalization, 118
critical race theory, 33, 111, 114
culpable negligence, 111
cultural processes, 28
culture, 2, 4, 6, 11, 14, 24, 30, 35, 48, 85, 89, 108
culture of poverty 2, 11

death penalty, 3, 12

## Index

deaths, 37–38, 88, 117–24
Declaration of Independence, 13, 16, 36–37, 99
dehumanization, 11, 16, 38, 96
Delaney, Martin, 68
democracy, 7, 17, 35–36, 38, 73, 122
dimensions of white supremacy, 30
disability, 52, 77
disabled veterans, 77
discrimination, 6, 17, 23, 26, 47, 57, 70, 75, 85–86, 88, 104–07
discrimination continuum, 26
disparity, 112
Distinguished Service Cross, 69
diversity, 23, 35, 59, 101, 103, 105–06, 109–10, 114
dominant racial group, 2, 4, 11, 22, 34–35, 39, 65, 89, 118
double-consciousness, 23
Double-V Campaign, 71
Douglas, Frederick, 16–17, 95–96
Du Bois, W. E. B., 16–17, 22–23, 28, 37, 46–48, 49, 82
duped, 1, 10–12, 16, 18–20, 43, 45, 57, 67, 80, 82–83, 96, 101, 103, 111, 115

economic downturns, 37
education, 2–3, 6–8, 10, 17, 22, 34–35, 40, 45–46, 49, 60, 64, 75, 77, 84, 90, 105, 107, 114
educational and penal realism, 34–35, 40
educational leaders, 2
Election 2020, 20, 117–124
emergency savings, 49, 63
employment, 17, 45, 48–49, 61, 77, 90, 103–04, 107
enslavement period, 7, 17, 26, 50–55, 57, 67–68
Equal Protection Clause, 54, 105
Equality, 6–7, 19, 23, 31–33, 35, 40–41, 43, 45–49, 60–65, 80, 82–83, 93, 104, 107, 109–10
equity, 35, 41, 49, 61, 65, 101, 103, 109–10

estate planning, 57
ethical individualism, 63
Evers, Medgar, 73
Executive Order 8802, 107
Executive Order 10479, 107
Executive Order 10925, 103
Executive Order 11246, 104, 107
extremist, 18, 91, 123

Fair Housing Act of 1968, 10, 84
fairness, 7, 38
Fanon, Franz, 22, 25, 31, 79
Farmer, JC, 81
farms, 17, 46, 51, 57, 59, 62
Farrakhan, Louis, 83–84, 98–101
Federal Bureau of Investigation, 7, 123
Federal Home Loan Bank Act, 59
Federal Housing Administration, 58–60
Ferguson, Missouri, 108
financial literacy, 64
First Amendment, 122
*Fisher v. University of Texas*, 106
Flint, Michigan, 118
Flood, Curt, 42
Floyd, George, 7, 20, 37–40, 99–101, 103, 108–14
formalists, 32
Forman, James, 63
Fourteenth Amendment, 32, 54, 105
Fourth of July, 16, 114
Frazier, E. Franklin, 22–25
free agent, 39
French Air Force, 69
French Army, 69

Garvey, Marcus, 69, 83–85
gender, 107, 118
GI Bill, 74–78, 82
Glaude, Eddie, 1
*Gratz v. Bollinger (2000)*, 105
Great Depression, 58–60, 74
Great Migration, 57
Great Recession, 19, 49, 60–65, 86
Greatest Generation, 19, 67–82
*Gutter v. Bollinger (2003)*, 106

harassment, 26
Hawaii, 70–71
Hawkins, Abe, 50–51
health, 2–5, 9, 37, 41, 48, 60–61, 98, 118, 120
health care, 2–4, 37, 118, 120
health outcomes, 118
heir property ownership, 57
Higgs, Lucy, 68
higher education, 3, 60
Historically Black Colleges and Universities, 76
Home Owner's Loan Corporation, 59–60
homeownership, 3, 8–9, 46, 61, 67
*Hopwood v. University of Texas (1996)*, 105–06
Hoover, J. Edgar, 59
hope, 1, 9–12, 16–19, 22, 54, 56, 69, 76, 78, 80, 82, 84, 87, 95, 98, 100–03, 108–115, 122–24
housing, 3, 9–10, 35, 48–49, 58–59, 71, 78–79, 84
Hurricane Katrina, 119

ideological processes, 28
Illinois, 117
immigrants, 27, 36–37, 123
inauguration address, 12–13
incarceration, 8, 11, 54, 61
inclusion, 1, 86, 101, 103, 109–10
income, 2–3, 45–47, 49, 60
individualism, 63, 88
industrial period, 27
inferiority, 2, 79, 88, 92, 96–97
inheritance, 3, 49, 52
Initiative 200, 105
institutional racism, 6, 19, 22, 96
insurrection, 117, 123
internal colonialism, 22, 28
International Black Appeal, 63

Jackson, Jesse, 21
James Meredith Freedom March, 87
James, LeBron, 42

Jamestown, Virginia, 1, 50
Jim Crow, 29, 80
Johnson, Henry, 69–70
Johnson, Hugh, 81
Johnson, Lyndon B., 104
Johnson, Magic, 42
justice, 7, 16–22, 27, 33–35, 38–39, 45, 63, 65, 72, 86–87, 91, 95, 98, 108–11

Kaepernick, Colin, 39, 109
Kennedy, John F., 12–13, 88, 103–04, 107
King Holiday, 87
King, Martin Luther, 10, 16, 18, 38, 42, 72, 83–95
knee, 113
Korean Conflict, 73
Ku Klux Klan, 71, 81, 93

land ownership, 55–57, 62
law enforcement, 7, 90–91, 100, 108, 118
lawful duty, 112
legal realists, 32
legitimizing ideologies, 107–08
lending, 49, 60–61
liberation, 7, 63, 67, 97–98, 100, 118, 122
life chances, 1, 26, 45, 87
Life Tabernacle Church, 121
Lincoln, Abraham, 13, 68, 88
loan forgiveness, 63
loans, 8–9, 59–61, 63, 75–76
Long, Charles, 15, 33, 36–37
Looters, 110
Louisiana, 9, 50–56, 71–72, 81, 117, 120–21
lynching, 17, 37, 69–70, 75, 79–81, 92, 115

Major League Baseball, 42
Make America Great Again, 99
mandates, 118
*Marco DeFunis, Jr. v. University of Washington Law School (1974)*, 106

Marshall, Thurgood, 31
Martin, Trayvon, 12, 20, 101, 108–09
Marxism, 22, 26, 87
masks, 118
mass incarceration, 11, 61
media, 3, 5–6, 21, 40, 60, 81, 94, 121–23
memorandum opinion, 111
Memorial Day, 13
mentoring, 4
metalanguage, 27
Miami Heat, 109
Michigan Freedom Fund, 121
middle class, 25–27
Midwest, 111, 118
military, 4, 8, 54, 55, 67, 69–71, 74–76, 80, 82, 121
military service, 4, 8, 67, 75, 80, 82
Minneapolis, Minnesota, 103
Minnesota Sentencing Guidelines, 112
Minnesota State Bar Association, 108–09
miscegenation, 9, 24
mobilization, 14, 85, 89, 92
mobs, 17, 58, 79–81
model minorities, 64
Montgomery Bus Boycott, 10, 72, 84
Moore, Stephen, 121
Morrison, Toni, 16
mortality, 4, 117
mortgages, 48–49, 58–60, 64
Mother Plane, 98
Mother Wheel, 98–99
Mothers of the Movement, 12
muscular assimilation, 119
myths, 16–19, 23–24, 29, 41, 47–58, 64, 67–82, 86, 93, 98, 106–07, 119

NAACP, 12, 31, 60, 76
Nation of Islam, 83, 84, 99, 101
National Basketball Association, 108–09
national covenant, 78
National Football League, 39, 87, 109
NCAA, 5–6
Neely, James, 81

Negro-complex, 24
Neighborhoods, 4, 49, 59–60, 65, 72, 93, 118
New Deal, 25, 58–60
New Negro Movement, 72–73
New York, 4, 12, 62, 64, 70–71, 117, 120, 123
Nixon, Richard, 104
Nonwhite, 12, 26, 29, 38, 56, 105–106, 114, 119
normalist school, 24
North, 17, 26, 53, 73
North Carolina, 5, 46, 81

Obama, Barack, 1, 11–12, 15, 21, 86, 107
offender, 104, 112–13
offense, 81, 112
opioid epidemic, 119
opportunity, 1, 8, 12, 17, 19, 26, 45–66, 68, 79, 87, 89, 94, 99, 103–106
oppression, 11, 16, 25–26, 31, 34–37, 67, 88–89, 91, 93–95
Ordinance 222, 9, 72
organic school, 24
outcomes, 2, 4, 20, 34–35, 41, 42, 82–83, 93, 101, 107, 118
overrepresentation, 3, 5, 16, 34–35, 37, 58, 60, 73, 117–18

pandemic, 37, 63, 84, 99, 111, 117–24
Parks, Rosa, 121
pathology, 23–25, 85, 119
patriotism, 114
peaks of panic, 86
peaks of progress, 40, 86
Pearl Harbor, 70–71
penalties, 106
pension, 68
performative act, 110
personal protective equipment, 118
*Philadelphia Negro*, 23
physical confrontation, 26
physical threats, 26
Pledge of Allegiance, 38

police, 7, 12, 18, 22, 25–26, 37–39, 42, 51, 58, 70, 81, 90, 92–94, 100–101, 103, 108–13, 115, 123
police brutality, 7, 18, 38, 109, 115
police shootings, 7
political elites, 1
political mobilization, 89
political modernization, 96
politics, 15, 22, 73, 85, 97
portfolio, 61
Post-Traumatic Stress Disorder, 4
poverty, 2–5, 11, 18–19, 43, 45, 47–48, 92–93,
power, 5, 17–18, 28–29, 32, 42, 48, 82–101, 110, 112, 114–15, 122, 124
pre-existing health conditions, 118
prejudice, 23–25, 28, 71
presumptive guidelines, 112
prison, 2, 11, 34, 40, 111–12, 120
Proposition 54, 90
Proud Boys, 123
public policy, 33, 55
public safety, 105, 112
Purple Heart, 69, 71

quotas, 104–06

race relations, 16, 22, 24–25, 40, 72
race-neutral, 30, 40, 75, 77, 88–89, 92–93, 105
racial achievement gap, 2
racial contacts, 24–25
racial disparities, 1–7, 34, 37, 40, 46, 49, 82, 89–90, 118
racial formation, 19, 22, 28
racial groups, 2, 4, 11, 22, 34–35, 89, 96, 118
racial identity, 23, 26
racial inegalitarianism, 30
racial justice, 36, 39, 109
racial oppression, 25, 28, 67, 88
racial prejudice, 23–25, 71
Racial Privacy Initiative, 90
racial realism, 1, 19–43, 45, 65, 67, 82–84, 101, 103, 114, 117, 124

racial reckoning, 100, 112
racial status quo, 25, 34, 70, 72, 79, 86, 91, 100
racial uplift, 27
racial wealth gap, 3, 19, 49, 61, 63–65
racialized social system, 1, 15, 28–29, 31, 34, 64, 79–80, 83–86, 91, 106
racism, 6, 11, 15, 19–20, 22, 26, 28–30, 32, 34, 40–42, 57, 60, 69–71, 73–75, 79, 88–89, 94, 96–98, 109–10, 114, 117–18
Rainbow Coalition, 21
rape, 71, 73, 91
realist school, 24, 32
Reconstruction, 8, 10, 19, 27, 43, 45, 54–58, 79, 98
redlining, 59, 118
reform, 34–35, 90, 97, 111
religion, 12–17, 21, 31, 36–43, 83–89, 91, 93, 98, 118
religious nationalism, 14, 85
religious realism, 39–43
reparations, 3, 61–64, 88
Republican Party, 12, 118, 121, 123
residential segregation, 22, 35, 40, 60
resigned acceptance, 26
resource mobilization, 89
respectability, 22
retirement accounts, 49, 61
*Ricci v. Destefano (2008)*, 106
riots, 58, 70–71, 110, 123
rituals, 13, 23, 38–39, 85
Roberts, Needham, 69
Roosevelt, Theodore, 76, 107, 119
Rough Riders, 9
Rowland, Dick, 58, 70

sanctions, 36, 93, 104, 112
Save Our Country Coalition, 121
savings, 49, 61, 63–64
schools, 2, 5–6, 24–26, 31–32, 34–35, 40, 42, 46–48, 58, 61, 68, 72, 74, 81, 86, 93, 105–06, 115
Second Amendment, 119
second generation immigrants, 27

Second Reconstruction, 10
second-degree manslaughter, 111
second-degree murder, 111
segregation, 9, 18, 22, 25, 31, 35, 40, 60–61, 72–74, 76, 79, 92
segregatory realism, 34
self-integrity, 35, 40
sentence, 2, 111–12, 114
sentencing, 111–13
sentencing disparity, 112
sentencing order, 111
Serviceman's Readjustment Act of 1944, 76–78
sickle cell anemia, 119
slavery, 13, 17, 25–26, 30–31, 42, 47, 50–55, 64, 69, 85, 91, 114
Smalls, Robert, 68
Smith, Tommie, 109
social heredity, 24
social justice, 18, 20, 27, 45, 86–87, 95, 101, 109–101
social relations, 24, 29, 48
social-psychological interventions, 2
socialism, 48, 62
sociology, 14, 22, 27
South, 2, 6–7, 17, 24, 26, 47, 53, 56, 63, 68, 71–72, 75–77, 80
South Carolina, 68
Southeastern Conference, 5
Spanish-American War, 73, 81
Special Field Order #15, 57
Spell, Tony, 121
sports, 5–6, 10, 22, 36, 38–42, 108, 114–15
status quo, 25, 34, 70, 72, 79, 86, 90–91, 100
stereotypes, 2, 23, 119
stock ownership, 61
strategic assimilation, 27
structural barriers, 118
struggle, 10, 19, 33, 43, 48, 55, 65, 67, 97, 109, 119
student loans, 63

subordination, 1, 3, 16–17, 19–21, 26, 33, 42–43, 80, 82, 95–101, 111, 114–15, 124
subprime loans, 49
symbolic assimilation, 27
symbols, 13, 38–39, 85, 88, 98

tax sales, 57
test scores, 2
The Criterion, 84, 99–101
*The Mystery,* 68
third–degree murder, 111
Thompson, William, 73
Three-Fifths Compromise, 26, 101
Till, Emmett, 10
Tricare, 4
Trump, Donald, 12, 37, 99–100, 108–09, 121, 123
trust, 71, 98, 109, 112
Ture, Kwame, 28, 83–101
Turpin, John Henry, 70
Tuskegee Airmen, 70
Twin Cities, 111

U.S. Air Force, 69, 104
U.S. Army, 69, 73, 75, 104
U.S. Army Air Service, 69
U.S. Capitol, 20, 117, 122–23
U.S. Department of Agriculture, 57
U.S. Marines, 69
U.S. Navy, 68–69, 75, 81, 104
*U.S. v. Paradise,* 105
U.S. War Department, 68
UFO, 83–94, 98
unemployment, 3, 49, 59, 75
unintentional second–degree murder, 111
United Negro Allied Veterans of America, 77
Universal Negro Improvement Association, 69
unreasonable force, 112
unreasonable risk, 111

vaccine, 100

verbal confrontation, 26
Veterans Health Administration, 4
victim, 7–8, 15, 17, 60, 62, 112–13, 118–19
video, 114
Vietnam War, 14, 79
violence, 15, 17, 41–42, 53–54, 79–80, 90–91, 108, 111, 114
vocational training, 75–76
voluntary sales, 57
Voting Rights Act of 1965, 10, 84, 88
vouchers, 6
vulnerable, 4–16, 31, 37

Wagner Act, 107
Washington, DC, 70, 120, 122
Washington, George, 13
wealth, 2–3, 8–9, 19, 25, 43, 45–50, 55, 58–75, 74, 93, 115
wealth gap, 3, 19, 49, 61, 63–65
welfare, 11, 49, 61–65
West, Cornel, 1
white backlash, 56, 90–101
White Citizen Council, 93
white racial frame, 19, 22, 34–35
white religious shock, 120
white supremacy, 29–31, 33, 37, 54, 73, 79–80, 110
white virtual mobs, 94
whiteness, 15, 25–27, 29–30, 33, 37–42, 55, 86, 89, 91, 94, 119, 121–22
whiteness as property, 26–27
Williams, Hosea, 80
withdrawal, 26
World War I, 69–70, 80–81
World War II, 19, 25, 67, 70–74, 76–80
*Wygant v. Jackson Board of Education,* 105

# About the Author

**Dr. Lori Latrice Martin** is association dean in the College of Humanities and Social Sciences and professor in the Department of African and African American Studies at Louisiana State University. Dr. Martin is the author of numerous books and scholarly articles. Dr. Martin's recent publications include: *Introduction to Africana Demography* and *America in Denial.* She was born and raised in Nyack, New York. She currently lives in Gonzales, Louisiana.

www.ingramcontent.com/pod-product-compliance
Lightning Source LLC
Chambersburg PA
CBHW061718300426
44115CB00014B/2734